The Remarkable Healing Power of

Velvet Antler

Nature's Link to:

Arthritis Relief
Vitality
Growth Factors
Sexual Function
Immune Enhancement
Athletic Performance

Betty Kamen, PhD
and
Paul Kamen

Nutrition Encounter, Novato, California

All of the facts in this book have been very carefully researched and have been drawn from the scientific literature. In no way, however, are any of the suggestions meant to take the place of advice given by physicians. Please consult a medical or health professional should the need for one be indicated.

In some cases, the names associated with the anecdotal stories have been changed to preserve privacy. The original testimonies are on file.

1999

Nutrition Encounter
PO Box 5847
Novato, CA 94948-5847
(415) 883-5154

Printed in the United States of America
First Printing 1999

ISBN 0-944501-13-3

DEDICATED TO

My Grandchildren
who spark my youth
and make me glad
I feel so young...

Tony Goldmark
Adaire Elizabeth Kamen
Rocky Kamen-Rubio
Emma Sabrina Kamen
Sarah Vick

Betty Kamen

ABOUT BETTY KAMEN

Years ago, on her popular radio program in New York City, Betty Kamen alerted her listeners to dozens of newly available supplements and treatments. Her program quickly developed into a center for disseminating new research and discoveries, featuring interviews with prominent alternative health care pioneers from around the world. Betty has written many cutting-edge health books, including the bestselling *Hormone Replacement Therapy, Yes or No? How to Make an Informed Decision.*

She received her MA in psychology in 1949, an MA in nutrition education in 1979, and her PhD in nutrition education in 1982. Betty taught at Hofstra University, developed a nutrition workshop at Stanford University Continuing Education Program for Doctors and Nurses, and served as nutrition consultant on the Committee of the Accrediting Council for Continuing Education and Training, Washington, DC.

A columnist for eight health news publications over the years, Betty has had more than 500 health reports published. Articles written by or about Betty have appeared in the *New York Times, Chicago Tribune, San Francisco Progress, Prevention Magazine*, *Baltimore Sun*, and many other local and national publications. A full page photo of Betty and one of her grandchildren appeared in a March 1998 issue of *Time Magazine*.

But never mind all the credentials. Betty says her children describe her most aptly when they say, “Mom? She’s just the oldest health nut in the country” — to which Betty responds: “If you have to be the oldest anything, ‘health nut’ is not so bad.”

ABOUT PAUL KAMEN

Paul Kamen is a naval architect with degrees from Webb Institute of Naval Architecture and the University of California at Berkeley. In addition to consulting projects, he writes for a local sailing magazine and contributes research support and technical illustrations for his mom's books and articles.

Paul's interest in food-based nutritional supplements stems from a very early exposure to brewer's yeast tablets and blackstrap molasses, part of every breakfast in the Kamen household since the early 50s.

Paul, Casilda, and Rocky now live 900 feet above sea level in Berkeley, California, where their hillside garden supports the local deer population with a variety of ornamental plants and organic vegetables.

ACKNOWLEDGMENTS

We wish to acknowledge those who have been so helpful and encouraging. Special thanks to:

Michael E. Rosenbaum, MD
Peter McNeary
Kelli Warriner
Don Baird
Rob Pek
Si Kamen
North American Elk Breeders Association

BOOKS & TAPES BY BETTY KAMEN, PhD

BOOKS

~ Hormone Replacement Therapy: Yes or No?
How to Make an Informed Decision

~ Kamut
An Ancient Food for a Healthy Future

~ Everything You Always Wanted to Know About Potassium
But Were Too Tired to Ask

~ New Facts About Fiber
How Fiber Supplements Can Enhance Your Health

~ The Chromium Connection
Diet & Supplement Strategy for Blood Sugar Control

~ Startling New Facts About Osteoporosis
Why Calcium Alone Does Not Prevent Bone Disease

~ Germanium
A New Approach to Immunity

~ Siberian Ginseng
Up-to-Date Research on the Fabled Tonic Herb

~ Sesame—The Superfood Seed
How It Can Add Vitality to Your Life

~ Nutrition In Nursing—The New Approach
A Handbook of Nursing Science

~ Osteoporosis
What It Is, How to Prevent It, How to Stop It

~ In Pursuit of Youth
Everyday Nutrition for Everyone Over 35

~ Kids Are What They Eat
What Every Parent Needs to Know About Nutrition

~ Total Nutrition for Breast-Feeding Mothers

~ Total Nutrition During Pregnancy
How To Be Sure You and Your Baby Are Eating the Right Stuff

TAPES

~ Lessons in Nutrition: Table Talk Tapes (Audio)
Topics covered in this landmark series: Supplements, Food & Immunity, Antioxidants (OPCs or Pycnogenol), Memory, Osteoporosis, Remedies.

~ Locker Room Logic: For Men Only
Preventing & Reversing Prostate Problems

~ Hormone Replacement Therapy
Audio & Video Tapes

~ Nutrition Breakthroughs
Six-pack Audio Series, Supplement Oriented

CONTENTS

FOREWORD

I became aware of velvet antler several years ago while browsing in a Chinese herbal shop in San Francisco. The product was marketed both by itself and in combination with ginseng. Somehow I felt an aura of mystery about powdered antlers sold in an obscure shop in Chinatown. Although skeptical when the proprietor said that velvet antler is very healing and that it would give me strength and energy, I felt compelled to buy some.

Indeed, a brief trial of velvet antler capsules proved his point. In just a few days I experienced a noticeable boost in my sense of general well being. This made me wonder why velvet antler was not being sold in health food stores or discussed in nutrition magazines. After all (as I subsequently learned), it is regarded in China as a precious healing substance and revered to the same degree as ginseng and perhaps Reishii mushroom.

Well, all that is about to change. I now know that velvet antler contains a veritable arsenal of nutritional weapons against diseases associated with aging. At last, velvet antler is beginning to receive the prominence and attention it deserves in the western world. In fact, it is poised to become one of the most exciting whole-food nutrition supplements of the new millennium.

Velvet antler, or simply "velvet" as it is commonly called, is an adaptogen. This means it has the ability to normalize many body functions that are out of balance. In China, maintaining the energy or *chi* in a state of balance is the primary goal of healing. Velvet has been used in Asia for thousands of years to enhance energy, stamina, endurance, stress tolerance, wound healing, mental capacity, and the growth of children. It also has been used to relieve sexual dysfunction, arthritis and soft tissue inflammation, insomnia, and dizzy spells.

The most familiar and coveted property of velvet is its ability to stimulate libido and enhance sexual performance. Most of its other healing properties are not as well known by the public. *The Remarkable Healing Power of Velvet Antler* is not at all limited to sexual function as it meticulously uncovers a broad range of velvet's therapeutic properties with a central focus on arthritis and soft tissue inflammation.

Connective tissue, the supporting matrix that literally holds our body parts together, has been a popular subject in recent years. Glucosamine and chondroitin sulfate have been used liberally for joint aches and pains and for arthritis. Betty and Paul wisely point out that velvet antler is richly endowed with chondroitin sulfate and with small proteins called growth factors that turboboost the creation of the carbohydrate polymers forming connective tissue. Ah yes! You will learn all about these carbohydrate polymers and their ability to maintain healthy tendons, ligaments, joints, and bones. You will find it easier to comprehend how velvet antler can play a vital role in preserving healthy connective tissue.

Betty Kamen and Paul Kamen have done exhaustive research perusing the ancient and modern literature. I have always been impressed by the simple, straightforward way Betty conveys the facts. There's no skimping in her messages, which is part of her formula for success as a noted nutritionist and author.

Together, Betty and Paul offer complete, comprehensive, well-researched scientific information, yet still retain warmth and humor. You feel they are talking directly to you about something important. And they are. It behooves everyone to pay attention.

Michael E. Rosenbaum, MD

Chapter 1

Overture

This book is about the future — an exciting and unparalleled new direction of the future of medicine. We refer to the fact that natural substances are beginning to find their way into the doctor's bag of treatments as we enter the new millennium. But the story we are about to tell is embedded in the past.

When there were no books or Internet to learn from, lessons came from life, with the wisdom of the ages related orally. And in the long-ago knowledge pertaining to health, the use of *velvet antler* was paramount.

You may well ask: "Is this something to add to my already long list of *here-we-go-again, try-this-old-remedy-and-see-if-it-works* supplements — or is this something different?" After reading the facts, you may be better able to make that decision.

My curiosity was tweaked when a health care practitioner said to me, after returning from an international Anti-Aging Conference, "The hot topic for the twenty-first century is *velvet antler*."

This inspired us to examine the world's production statistics of velvet antler.

Annual Production of Velvet Antler

New Zealand	450 tons
China	400 tons
Russia	80 tons
United States	20 tons
Canada	20 tons

~~~

Korea is the largest consumer of processed velvet antler products and the largest exporter, grossing approximately 1.6 billion dollars (US) in annual sales.

What's going on? What should we know about the forces propelling these sales? Here are a few more facts:

In China and Korea, velvet antler has always been and still is used across a broad spectrum of therapeutic and preventive applications, with children in Korea receiving ten percent of the total consumption.[1]

More than 250 articles have been published on the manufacture, composition, and biochemical effects of velvet antler.
~~~

Clinical experience prompted Michael Rosenbaum, MD, to state:

> *"Velvet antler contains the missing link to longevity, something just not present in all the promising nutrition programs I have ever worked* with. *Its growth factors are a significant part of what makes it so special. Growth factors may be the only substances that can retard and even reverse aging."*[2]

Research points to velvet antler's ability to reduce the inflammation and pain of arthritis by addressing the real causes of this disease, something modern medicine has not been able to accomplish.

We have been impressed with the antler's unique lipid and amino acid profiles, its unusual protein-sugar factions, its influence on hormone metabolism, and its anabolic agents. Those who have studied the literature on velvet antler predict that other elements of consequence in this imposing product are yet to be identified.

A wise practitioner, an octogenarian who still makes house calls, said: "It's the *gestalt*, the totality — the fast-growing, life-infused entire package that explains the unusual power of velvet antler."

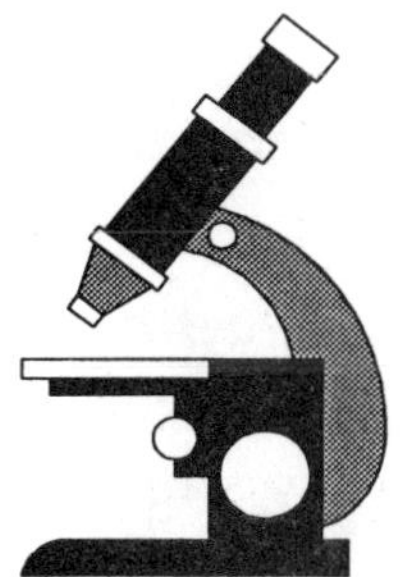

The Antler and the Placenta

The only other mammalian organ that grows and is discarded in nine months (and can grow again in the same mammal) is the placenta. Growth of an organ requires energy and a system whereby super nutrient raw materials must flow to that developing organ. This challenges all the efficiency and complexity that nature ever devised. Both the placenta and the antler have an amazing spectrum of cellular and biochemical activity that includes cell replication, immune mechanisms, and unique aging processes — *accelerated and intensified because of their short life cycles.*

Just as the placenta has singular substances needed for nourishment for its own particular metabolism as it grows to senescence, so it is with the antler. Not unlike the placenta, some dynamic entity in the growing antler regulates and controls the concentration ratios of the special nutrients necessary for its purposeful development.

And both are shed after a defined period, in balance with the host.

Perhaps we'll never fully understand what propels the mechanisms that end the pregnancy or discard the antler. We all know the placenta is essential to the survival of the fetus. In an expansive (and perhaps slightly exaggerated) sense, the antler also contributes to the continuation of life, particularly for the elk in the wild.

It provides superiority to the male during the fall mating season. The female species that grow antlers use them as weapons for forays in food competitions during pregnancy.[3]

Broad-based Applications

No one knows when velvet antler was first used for medicinal purposes. The written record in China goes back about two thousand years to a silk scroll found in a tomb. There is every reason to believe that it was considered an age-old tradition even then.

You can almost hear Ancient Mom saying to Ancient Child, "Your wise Grandma taught me about the velvet antler. Her wise grandma taught her.

Or perhaps Ancient Mom said to Ancient Child, just as our mothers said to us when dispensing cod liver oil: "Stop fussing. This is for your own good. It will keep you healthy."

Velvet antler has been thought of as a tonic in the traditional sense of the word — a substance that is both protective and curative. Ancient Mom may also have known that it was used historically for anemia, arthritis, impotence, uterine bleeding, dizziness, insomnia, amnesia, wounds, and pain — validated by prescriptions cited in historical medical texts from China and Korea.[4,5]

We tend to think of traditional Chinese practice as being heavily oriented toward herbal medicine, but in fact animal products have always played an important role therapeutically. The best-known historical reference to velvet antler is the Grand Materia Medica of 1596 by Li Shi-Zhen. Of the 1,892 medicinal substances cataloged, 444 of them are animal products.

Velvet antler is now considered the second most important ingredient in traditional Chinese medicine (after ginseng).

In that early written record that goes back two millennia, it is claimed that this remarkable substance alleviates fifty-two illnesses. And now we have the science to validate the folklore.

Because of its very specific and extraordinary bioactivity and chemical components, velvet antler has been shown to help divert a variety of today's diseases to their demise. It can increase the oxygen-carrying capacity of the blood, extend an athlete's endurance limit and performance, and improve mental capacity. Chinese students take velvet antler while studying for exams.

Velvet antler's long history of effective use as a treatment for sexual dysfunction initially caused it to be classified as an aphrodisiac by western physicians studying eastern medicine. Some researchers have suggested that this delayed the investigation of other uses, and may explain why such a potent therapeutic substance has taken so long to become popularized in North America.

Antler has been used with reported success against impotence, watery semen, and other sexual dysfunction. As for libido, the long-term tonic action has been stipulated to have an eventual beneficial aphrodisiac result. Anecdotes about more immediate reactions also abound. And, as we will see, it has been scientifically demonstrated to increase testosterone levels in athletes.

Today, velvet antler is being used to encourage:

~ arthritis relief
~ muscle development
~ increased strength
~ increased endurance
~ red blood cell production to correct anemia
~ capacity of blood to carry oxygen
~ speedy recovery from injury and stress
~ faster recuperation after surgery
~ augmented levels of certain anabolic hormones
~ enhanced immune activity
~ fertility

The North American elk (or wapiti) and the red deer are the two species now cultivated in North America for antler production. No significant differences have been found in the composition of the velvet antlers from these two breeds. In fact, velvet antler obtained from either the North American elk or red deer is chemically synonymous. It is utilized commercially for identical purposes.

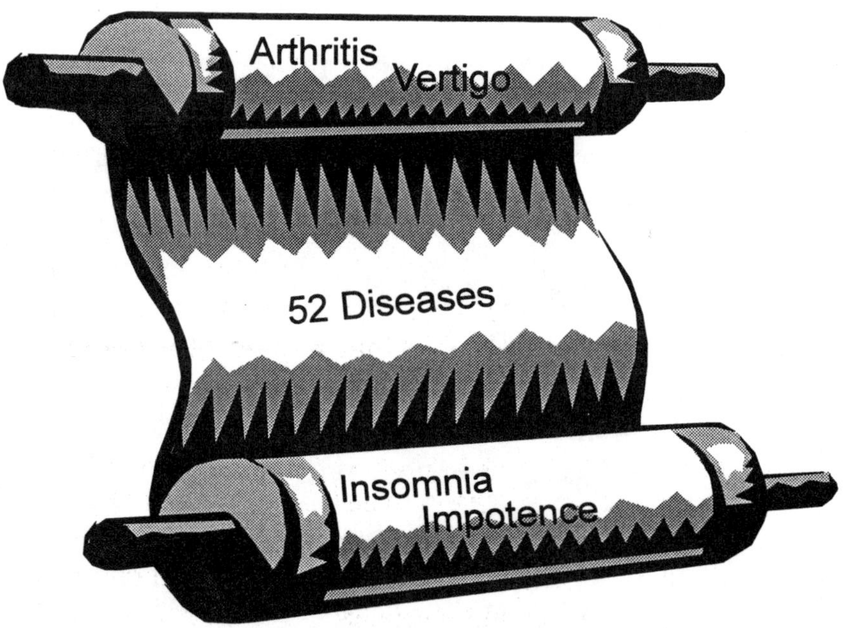

Taken together, ancient tradition and new research validating the benefits of velvet antler make a compelling case for its inclusion in every healthful diet.

A Letter from Rod McLeod

"On September 8, 1979, I was involved in a farm tractor accident that left me seriously injured with multiple leg fractures and internal injuries. In the next three years I had 51 operations and numerous experimental procedures required to repair the damages suffered in the accident. As I now enter my mid-thirties, the effects of the accident continue as arthritis and joint problems become more apparent.

"About a year and a half ago, I discovered elk velvet antler, a product that has provided considerable relief to my arthritis and joint problems.

"My worst pain area is my right knee. Because the break in my lower leg could not be properly aligned, tremendous amount of stress has been transferred to my knee. Doctors have already told me that the knee will have to be replaced, and advised that the longer I can wait for the procedure, the better, considering my age and the fact that a knee replacement will only last 15-20 years.

"I was amazed with the results after taking the velvet antler for only a couple of weeks. It substantially reduced the inflammation in the knee joint. I have now been taking velvet antler for over a year and can still report the same positive results. It's interesting that if I forget to take my 'pills' for a couple of days, not only does my knee quickly remind me of my pain, but the inflammation returns. I also notice little aches and pains in other parts of my body. I believe the use of elk velvet antler has given me significant pain relief and extended the time period before requiring major constructive knee surgery."

Dear Antler,
I have dieted. I have jogged. I have learned good-thought techniques. None of this has worked for my arthritis.

Signed, Still In Pain

Dear Still In Pain: Our environment has become too toxic for anyone to enjoy optimal health without some source of high-powered nutrient supplementation. Nutrition, hormones, illness, and experiences over a lifetime — including whether or not you were breast-fed — all etch their imprint. Continue to watch what you eat, try fast walking instead of running, and keep on thinking all those good thoughts. But now is the time to do one more thing: Add a nutrient-dense supplement or two to that list of great lifestyle habits.

Velvet antler is a good choice.

Chapter 2

From the Caldron to the Health Store

Velvet antler sounds like something that should go into the witch's caldron right after the eye of newt and just before the toe of frog. Mention an antler product as a food supplement, and most people in North America will conclude that you are on the far fringe of alternative nutrition.

Yes, they know that horns, antlers, and elephant tusks have been used for medicinal purposes for thousands of years. They might even know that some of these substances are still very much in demand, and in some cases this demand has even led to the tragic destruction of endangered populations.

But from a nutritional point of view, the popular perception is that these substances are made of more-or-less inert and lifeless material, valuable only for their mineral content. Surely these minerals could be obtained far more economically from less exotic sources.

For the uninformed, the belief that horns, teeth, and antlers have unique medicinal or therapeutic value requires that we accept a belief system that must reach far beyond the realm of rational nutritional science. How can something as dead as a powdered antler have any significant effect on human health?

The skeptics might be able to make a good case against tiger's teeth, but velvet antler is very different. The velvet antler is a fast-growing and biologically active tissue, loaded with collagen, amino acids, growth factors, prostaglandins, trace elements, choline, unique combinations of proteins and carbohydrates, and other substances whose structures are not yet identified. Those we have identified are nutrients that have been demonstrated by rigorous research to have exceptional therapeutic value.

The basic requirements for every living thing — plant or animal — tend to resemble each other. But just how these specific bioactive nutrients in velvet antler are used to the health advantage of humans *without harm to the source animal itself* is an extraordinary story.

What Is Velvet Antler?

Antlers are not to be confused with horns. The word antler is derived from the Latin *anteoculae*, which simply means “in front of the eye” (although the antler is actually behind the eye). Antlers grow on permanent pedestal-like projections from the animal’s skull. These protrusions are called *pedicles*. And unlike horns, antlers are cast off and regenerated every year. They are found on almost all cervids, the name given to members of the deer family. Cervids include elk (or wapiti), caribou, reindeer, and moose. Except for reindeer and caribou, only the stags (adult males) grow antlers.

Horns, on the other hand, are found on bovids — cattle, water buffalo, mountain goats, bighorn sheep, bison, and antelope. Horns don’t fall off every year. They are made of keratin, the same protein that helps to make hair, nails, and skin. Horns have none of the special properties of the biologically active velvet antler.

The pedicles and the first set of antlers develop in early spring of the stag’s first year, typically at ten months of age. Antler is made of *cartilage,* not keratin. Because of its rapid growth rate, it is a very biologically active tissue, well supplied with blood, covered with skin and a fine velvet-like layer of hair. At this stage of development the entire antler, not just the skin, is known as *velvet antler*.[1]

After several months of growth and development, the antler cartilage slowly turns to bone. The blood vessels and nerves diminish, and finally, the stag will scrape off any remaining skin and hair. This leaves a sharp bony structure that the animal uses to assert his superiority during the fall mating season. The female among the species that grow antlers use this weapon for forays in food competitions, especially during pregnancy.[2]

Each spring, the old set of antlers is cast off and the cycle begins again. Support tissues such as nerves are recreated along with new bone formation.[3]

> *Antlers are unique in that they are the only mammalian organs that regenerate annually.*

Velvet antler for human consumption is harvested before the velvet has started to turn to bone. The antler is cut off about a centimeter above the pedicle. (A centimeter is a little under one-half inch.) The remaining slice of antler, the part that isn't harvested, is called a button, and the button goes through the normal process of calcification. The button drops off next spring when new antlers begin to form, at about the same time the full antler set would have dropped off.

Harvesting the velvet should occur about halfway through the antler's growth cycle, typically fifty-five to sixty days after "button drop." After harvest, the velvet may be cooled, dried, and then frozen.

Those who have chosen vegetarianism for ethical reasons may take particular interest in velvet antler supplements.

> *Velvet antler is a potent nutritional product obtained without detriment to the animal.*

Securing velvet for human use without harm to the animal is something unequalled by any other animal-derived food, with the exception of milk and eggs. The New Zealand Game Industry Board claims that antlers are removed using "a humane process that causes no stress or injury."[4] Compare this to the horrors of the slaughterhouse!

On farms where the animals are well cared for, with plenty of everything to answer their needs, can we assume that the antler does not serve the elk as it would in the wild? Dr. Lindsay Matthews, a prominent animal behaviorist, has studied stags in detail before and after removal of the antler. He confirms that those with antlers removed are far less likely to damage themselves or each other. He observed the usual grazing patterns among the animals with or without their antlers. He did not see any discernible differences in heart rates or stress levels.[5]

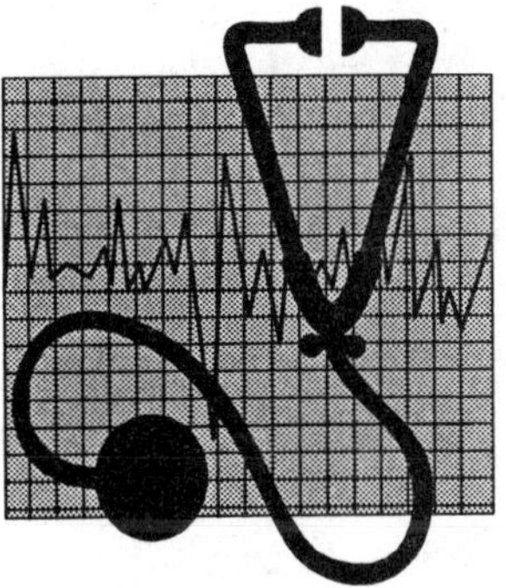

Recently, an old belief was scientifically disproved: The blood supply in the antler bone is *not* interrupted at any stage, even as it solidifies. The finding of bone-building cells in the pedicle, with a rich supply of capillaries and vessels, indicates continuous bone remodeling and a well-developed vascular system — despite the presence of hard antler bone. This does indeed represent living bone.[6]

The value of the velvet changes as the cartilage begins to calcify into bone. The more "bony" the antler, the less benefit it has in the marketplace. The transition occurs over time at any one location on the antler, and also varies from tip to base.[7]

Many important substances distinguish velvet antler from other products. The specific list of components, described later, characterize the complexity of this unusual substance. To make it even more complicated, some of the vocabulary is new to most of us. If we are to understand how velvet antler does what it does, words like *glycosaminoglycans* (abbreviated GAGs) and *proteoglycans* need to be defined.

Specific nutrients rarely perform their individual miracles alone. All of our working parts are intricately connected to all other working parts. That's why we stand firm, repeating the message that the use of very special — and sometimes hard-to-come-by — substances provided by nature are far superior to isolated elements, whether synthetic or natural. Velvet antler is a prime example of such a product.

Some distant day, as the interior of our cells become more approachable with new advances in technology, we will undoubtedly reveal more of velvet's secrets. Our enthusiasm for fully understanding every nuance makes us wish we could set our watches ahead a few decades. But as with so many other working therapies, alternative or traditional, those who suffer need not wait for the incomplete science to catch up with the results.

~~~

These intriguing questions were presented in an article titled, "Future Directions in Antler Research":

~ By what developmental processes are antlers able to prescribe their own morphogenesis with mirror image accuracy year after year?

~ Why do healing pedicle stumps give rise to antler buds instead of scar tissue?

~ How do the elk find enough calcium to make such massive antlers in only a few months?

~ How could these improbable appendages have evolved mechanisms to commit suicide, jettison the corpse, and regenerate new ones every year?[8]
~~~

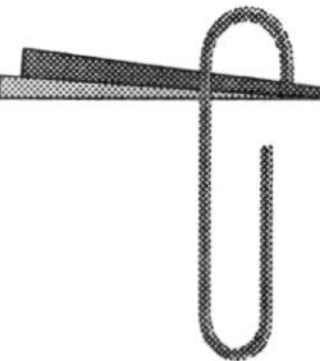

Dear Antler:

I've been a strict vegan for most of my adult life. I know I can get all the nutrients I need without having to eat animal products. Yet I keep hearing that there are things in velvet antler that I can't get from any vegetable sources, Is there a vegetarian alternative?

Signed, Searching For Truth

Dear Searching: Vegetarians are generally way ahead of the curve compared with the "normal" US diet. But if you study aboriginal cultures worldwide, you're not likely to find any example of one that totally excludes meat or fish as part of the traditional diet. I respect your choice to be a strict vegetarian. This is all the more reason you should consider an antler supplement, if you can come to terms with the fact that the animal gives up the antler a little sooner than nature intended. Yes, there are things in velvet antler that are difficult to get from non-animal sources.

The information about the benefits of velvet antler comes from biologic knowledge, not Madison Avenue "science by press release." The research behind it is very impressive. Good luck with your decision.

Chapter 3

History and Traditions of Velvet Antler for Health

The true goal of Asian medicine is for each person to learn the dynamics involved in maintaining their own good health. The doctor can only assist in the healing process, the most important work being done by the person through lifestyle adjustments. Would that we had such a philosophy in the American medical community!

The Yin-Yang Connection

In Chinese medicine velvet antler is at the top of the yang scale, aligned with masculinity. Remember that antler growth is part of the preparation for sexual competition. This is important because a large part of Chinese medicine deals with restoring the balance between yin and yang, and many of velvet antler's properties can be inferred from how it is used to do this.

For those who may not be familiar with the yin-yang concept, there are two principles in Chinese philosophy and religion from whose interaction all things are produced and all things are dissolved. One is negative, dark, and feminine — yin; and one is positive, bright, and masculine — yang. The two polar elements originally referred to the shady and sunny sides of a valley or a hill, but the concept developed into the relationship of any contrasting pair. The movement of energy between the two extremes are the yin and the yang. And the constant flux between the two poles can be observed in all things, from the smallest molecule to the pulsation of the galaxies.

Examples are female-male (specified above), cold-hot, wet-dry, weak-strong, and so on. One force moves toward the other, and the flux and the balance are thought to create well being. A deficiency of either principle can manifest as disease.

The philosophy is also encompassed in food. All foods have both yin and yang qualities, but a single food is predominantly one or the other. Each category is essential to health, so you must consume foods from each classification. Today's knowledge about the importance of variety in our foods reflects this philosophy. *To eat is to take in the whole environment.* One must wonder if or how our highly processed foods would ever be ranked, yin-yang style.

Yin-yang is not a distinct system of thought by itself but it permeates Chinese life: A balance of yin and yang is believed to be essential to health.

In the Marketplace

Nutrients vary in different sections of the velvet antler. No doubt observation led to applications of these different sectors for special purposes.

Here's a traditional method of antler preparation:
The velvet antler is cut into four pieces from base to tip, and each section is sliced further. The two upper sections, sometimes called the *wax pieces*, are used as preventive tonics for children and adolescents. The middle lower section, the *blood piece,* is used for arthritis and osteomyelitis (a disease of inflammation of bone, which may spread to involve the marrow, cortex, and more). The lower section, the base or bone piece, is designated as helpful for older people, especially if calcium deficiency needs to be corrected.

Traditional Chinese practice positions the velvet during drying so that blood drains out of the tip (hence the name wax piece, distinguishing it from velvet that maintains the blood). Other methods retain considerable blood in this part of the velvet.[1]

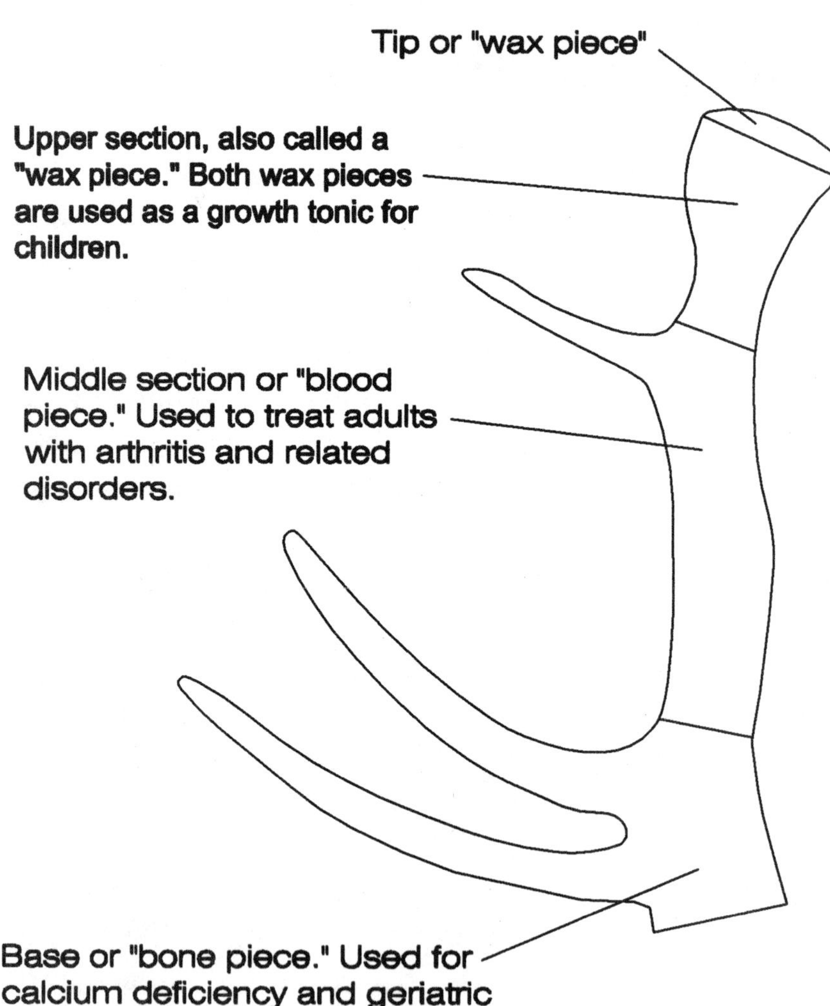
Parts of the velvet antler
and some traditional uses
Tip or "wax piece"
Upper section, also called a "wax piece." Both wax pieces are used as a growth tonic for children.
Middle section or "blood piece." Used to treat adults with arthritis and related disorders.
Base or "bone piece." Used for calcium deficiency and geriatric therapies.

FIGURE 1

A traditional Korean clinic processes the velvet in powder form, with distribution of four grams to a packet. A one-year-old is typically prescribed one packet per year, a three-year-old gets three per year, and adults are advised to take about twenty per year. Only one packet is prescribed to women in labor, in deference to the fetus, but its main purpose is to offer benefit for the delivery process.[2]

One purchasing routine is reminiscent of how our great-grandmothers shopped. The antler is sliced at the time of sale to the consumer. This method has advantages in terms of quality control because it allows both the seller and a knowledgeable buyer to assess value by observing size, color, smell, and appearance of the intact velvet antler stick.[3] Our great-grandmother gauged quality by examining these very features of the whole animal at the butcher's, or the condition of the fish eyes at the fish vendor's, even though she was purchasing only a very small part of the animal.

This is in sharp contrast to the extracts and powders in modern packaging where the identity of a nutritional supplement product may be in question. It's also a far cry from our current practice of buying parts of animals in the freezer bins at the supermarket. We have good reason to be concerned about the condition of the rest of the animal. Questions are raised based on marketing procedures we've investigated and have seen in documentaries.

In the absence of accepted uniform standards for origin, composition, and processing, the traditional distribution methods of velvet antler may continue to be favored by most of the Asian market.

The old-time butcher.

Pantocrin

Velvet antler was used in Russia in the fifteenth century, but its use as an aphrodisiac (along with animal horns) is considerably older. Organized farming for antlers in Russia, however, did not begin until about 1840.

As an example of how nebulous our supplement labeling has been, my family used a product called Pantocrin in the 1960s. Our nutrition-aware physician procured it for us, and we never questioned the derivation of the impressive nutrient breakdown list printed on the package. Now we know "the rest of the story": Pantocrin is essentially a total lipid extract of velvet antler.

Pantocrin was actually introduced in 1931. This was the first velvet antler product to be studied in detail, and it is still available today as tablets or ampules. Dosage recommendations vary according to indication and whether or not the product is being used with other therapy.

In the late 1960s, rulondin, a Japanese version of pantocrin, was introduced as an injectable treatment for male sexual disorders. Conclusions from research led to the formulation of the product in injection, capsule, and drink form. These preparations are mainly used as cardiovascular tonics.[4] Lu jung is yet another velvet antler product promoted to rejuvenate and provide added energy.

In the 1970s, it was shown that pantocrin was responsible for beneficial enzyme activities of the cervical cord in whiplash injury.[5] This was recently confirmed by the Elk Technical International Research Center.[6] (We cite information about nerve growth factors later on.)

We are now in awe of our physician's recommendation of pantocrin as an all-around tonic several decades ago. He was one of a small coterie of practitioners in this country who somehow was fully aware of nature's unusual secrets used in other countries for helping to unlock wellness.

Processing

The commercial method of processing velvet antler once involved boiling the antlers and then allowing them to dry at 60 to 70 degrees C. In 1974, Russian researchers demonstrated that boiling the antler tips destroyed much of their bioactive potential.[7] No surprises here. Then it was discovered that the drying process increased the potency of many of its active compounds.[8] Good news here.

Newer methods of extraction involve a freeze-drying process and do not require boiling.[9] Freeze-drying is commonly adopted to produce a dry and stable form of many different kinds of biological materials, offering protection from serious denaturing. Proteins are left in reasonably native form and the material can be stored without refrigeration for long periods.

Velvet antler processing technology continues to be explored. Recent developments from the University of Alberta have resulted in methods that can reduce the adverse effect on collagen caused by heating.[10]

And we continue to be fascinated by the melding of the old and the new.

PANTOCRIN RESEARCH

In 1969, it was shown that pantocrin increased the working capacity of test animals.

Breckhman, JT et al. 1969
Biological Series No. 10(2):112-115

In 1974, Russian scientists reported that athletes on an exercise cycle performed 15 kg/m of dynamic work, whereas those given pantocrin increased this to 74 kg/m. They also concluded that pantocrin showed marked antiinflammatory activity.

Yudin, AM and Dubryakov, YL 1974
Academy of Sciences of USSR, Far East Science Center, Vladivostock

Also in 1974, another Russian scientist showed that the beneficial action in athletes is primarily aimed at accelerating the restorative processes after intensive activity, and at increasing the body's resistance to unfavorable external influences.

Fulder, S, 1980
New Scientist 87(1215):516-519

Dear Antler,

My significant other and I are betting on whether velvet antler is a drug or a nutrient. What say you?

Signed, Hoping-To-Win

Dear Hoping-to-Win: Note this vocabulary in a recent medical journal report: "Oral chondroitin sulfate is an effective and safe symptomatic slow-acting drug for the treatment of knee osteoarthritis. In addition, chondroitin sulfate might be able to stabilize the joint space width and to modulate bone and joint metabolism, and influence the natural course of osteoarthritis in humans."

In its isolated form, science researchers perceive chondroitin sulfate as a drug. As part of velvet antler, it is a natural constituent. Since velvet antler is not an isolated substance, it can hardly be referred to as a drug. I hope you were on the winning side of this bet.

Reference: Uebelhart D et al. "Effects of oral chondroitin sulfate on the progression of knee osteoarthritis: a pilot study." *Osteoarthritis Cartilage* 1998 May;6 Suppl A: 39-46.

Chapter 4

How Does Velvet Antler Work?

Millennia rolled away and era followed era, yet a large number of our afflictions stayed with us. We seem to be surprised when we learn that today's common symptoms parallel agonies of ancient days. Arthritis is just such a disease. In fact, it's one of the oldest known disorders of human beings. The earliest recorded example in a vertebrate animal was discovered in the fossil skeleton of the platycarpus. This prehistoric and very large reptile lived about one hundred million years ago.

Before we attempt to explain how velvet works, let's note what it does *not* do: It is not antiviral or antibacterial, nor is it antifungal, and it will not cure an infectious disease condition — not directly, anyway. But keep in mind that healthy people are less likely to be infected with a pathogen. And if they do fall prey, symptoms are more mild and discharged more quickly.

> *Even pneumonia is a different disease when the immune system is badly compromised (or not).*

Soft Boundaries

The therapeutic effects of velvet antler seem to fall into several major categories:

~ antiinflammatory effects
~ anabolic growth properties
~ enhancement of immune response
~ anticancer effects

In researching these areas, it becomes extremely difficult to keep them separate. Substances believed to have a primary effect in one area turn out to be very helpful in another. Examples: In addition to their tissue-building role, growth hormone precursors found in velvet antler are important for immunity, and the antler's cartilage components are antiinflammatory as well as possible anticancer agents. The deeper we study, the more difficult it becomes to associate only one of the velvet antler's constituents with only one mode of action.

Adaptogens

Moreover, the component parts don't behave in a predictable or consistent way, in contrast to how a drug or pharmaceutical product is expected to perform. The active ingredients in velvet antler are mostly precursors, raw materials required by your body to process substances that maintain your good health. This is why their action is not drug-like, but *adaptogenic*, tending to correct whatever is out of balance, rather than forcing a physiological parameter in a particular direction.

> *Velvet works by allowing your natural control systems to move in the direction of normalcy.*

Like many adaptogenic nutrients, velvet antler appears to be effective against a very wide range of disorders. This is true of any therapy that addresses systemic health. An adaptogen appears to have no specific function — until it is needed. In other words, *it adapts to your needs*. It's like money in the bank, serving little purpose until you make a withdrawal.

Adaptogens are almost always user-friendly and are classified as nontoxic. They are known to enhance your ability to cope with any stress — physical, emotional, or chemical. They differ from drugs in several ways. No prescriptions are necessary. No high-tech equipment, needles, syringes, or professional expertise are required for administration. They are usually far less costly than drugs. They are not habit-forming. A drug continues to alter the physiology after a state of normalcy is achieved; an adaptogen, on the other hand, regulates, and is held in abeyance when the challenge ceases to exist.

> *The most important aspect of an adaptogen is that it is rarely found in nature as an isolated element.*

More likely, an adaptogen is a complex natural substance that works because your body is an intricate chemical factory, carrying out a multitude of highly elaborate chemical transformations.

> *We do not fully understand every nuance and subtlety of our life processes. That's why nature's adaptogenic substances in supplemental form have become a necessity in our efforts to combat our current toxic environment.*

The Whole, Rather Than the Parts

The result of the broad-spectrum mode of action for velvet has spawned a very extensive array of claims and recommendations.

A large body of data proves beyond any doubt that people who include more vegetables and fruit in their diets are healthier, stronger, smarter, and live longer. But the same cannot always be said for nutrient supplements. Although various studies demonstrate beneficial effects of single-ingredient vitamin therapy, there are those that show no effect. Why should this be, when the vitamins are the same substances believed to account for the health-promoting qualities of the foods they come from?

Two answers suggest themselves: The first is synergy.

> *Vitamins, minerals, antioxidants, and other nutrients work better in groups, as found in nature.*

The other and more crucial reason is the presence of unidentified cofactors. This acknowledges that there are many things about the constituency of healthful food that we still don't know, i.e., there's a lot more that we don't know than we do know.

For example, it is known that there are many kinds of carotene in the carotene complex. Yet beta-carotene gained popularity as a supplement. The other carotenes may well be equally important, or may even be vital in ways that beta-carotene alone cannot substitute. It has been speculated that this is one of the several reasons behind the negative results of the Danish beta-carotene study, in which heavy smokers fared slightly worse with beta-carotene supplements than without.[1] (It was also a case of too little, too late.) The fact is you don't find beta-carotene all by itself in nature. Nature makes carotene complex. And, like it or not, we are embedded in nature.

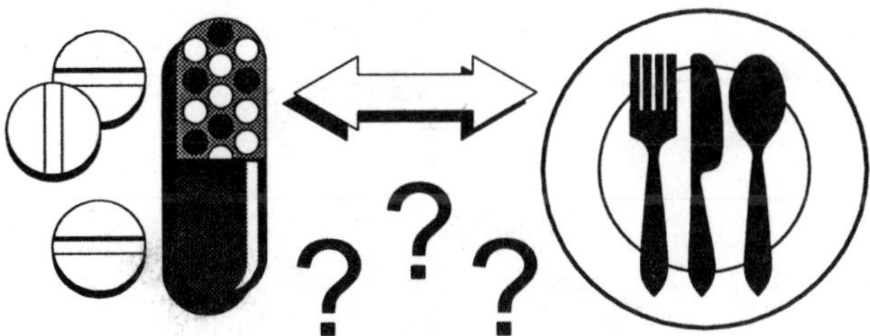

Another example involves the use of natural vitamin E from food compared with synthetic vitamin E supplementation in postmenopausal women. A recent study showed that those getting their vitamin E from food displayed significant reductions in LDL oxidation (the "bad-guy" cholesterol). Postmenopausal women who took synthetic vitamin E via supplements, however, experienced increased levels of this unwanted factor.[2]

An unclear force propels nature's assemblage of nutrients into purposeful union — each part influenced by the other parts. Despite the fact that technology allows us to zero in on smaller and smaller, we have yet to grasp all of the reasons for the success of the *gestalt,* the total picture.

Most recently, results from The Health Professionals Follow-up Study, a large research program involving more than 43,000 men failed to show any substantial association between consumption of vitamin E, vitamin C and carotenoids and the risk of ischemic or hemorrhagic stroke. "A diet rich in fruits and vegetables, however, is likely to reduce risk in most people," concluded the Harvard researchers.[3] (That doesn't mean these isolated nutrients may not be of value for other purposes.)

The lesson here is to get as much of your nutrients as possible from foods: *whole, fresh, raw, natural foods.*

> *Are you are ready to adopt the ascetic life of the true fanatic? If not, the culinary lifestyle just proposed for optimal health is very difficult.*

Needless to say, eating whole natural foods should still be your goal. But supplementation is a necessity if you expect to function in this modern world, no matter how exemplary your dietary choices.

Augmenting your nutrient intake can take several forms. Except for special needs, it doesn't have to be the single-substance vitamin, or even a large handful of isolated nutrients. Certain foods appear to be so rich in nourishment that they can be condensed into easy-to-take supplements without losing the chemical diversity that makes them so effective.

Velvet antler is one of these special foods. There is no single active ingredient that defines its quality, and we will probably never have a complete list of its components, or full explanations of how they accomplished what they are believed to do.

The following chapter describes what we do know about the substances in velvet antler at this time.

Dear Antler,

I open this jar, open that bottle, open the next bottle. I'm tired of doing this. How can I reduce the number of supplements I swallow with each meal?

Signed, Major Supplement Taker

Dear Supplement Taker: Velvet antler, handed down through decades of time, is currently used worldwide for protective and rejuvenating effects, and to help a long list of existing problems.

Anyway, that's the 1999 report right out of the Elk Technical International Research Center. Based on current studies, this could have merit! If we were to search for a single magic bullet for wellness, velvet antler would certainly be a top contender based on this imposing roll call. You might try velvet antler for awhile, and see if you notice a difference. Chances are, you will, and perhaps you can cut down on some of the other supplements.

Reference: Church, J.S. "Velvet antler: Its historical medical use, performance-enhancing effects and pharmacology." Elk Technical International Research Center. Website: http://www.elk-tech.com/research.htm. 1999.

Chapter 5

What's In Velvet Antler?

The information that follows is not necessarily meant to be studied, but rather scanned and used as a reference to clarify some of the concepts considered here.

The developing antler is comprised of a variety of cell types, including fibroblasts, chondroblasts, chondrocytes, and osteocytes. We don't mean to challenge your science with this terminology, but it helps to understand these words as we interpret velvet antler's role in its benefit for various disease states. Therefore, note this short (very short) lesson in etymology:

~ fibro refers to fiber
~ chondro refers to cartilage
~ osteo refers to bone
~ cyte simply means cell
~ blast refers to any cell yet to be defined, that is, yet to adapt to a particular function; an immature precursor of the type of cell indicated by the preceding prefix

So,

~ fibroblast is a cell that forms fibrous tissue
~ chondroblast is a cell that will form cartilage
~ osteoblast is a cell that will form bone
~ chondrocyte is a developed cartilage cell
~ osteocyte is an already-developed bone cell

And, just for the record, *clasis* refers to breaking up. The word osteoclast refers to cells that help to break up bone. (If you break a tooth, it's referred to as odontoclasis.)

Found in Velvet Antler

- *Amino acids*...Including essential amino acids, with a gradual increase in concentration from base to tip (any essential nutrient is one your body doesn't manufacture: you must eat it to get it.)

- *Linolenic acid*...The most significant of our essential fatty acids; required in higher amounts by humans than other fatty acids; found in tip only

- *Phospholipids*...The major structural lipids (fats) of most of our cellular membranes; includes lysophosphasidyl lysophosphatidyl choline, phosphatidyl choline; blood-pressure lowering function; anti-aging ben efits[1,2,3]

- *Minerals*...Mostly calcium, phosphorus, magnesium, iron, and potassium, some of which increase as antler hardens

- *Collagen*...Protein substance of the fibers of skin, tendon, bone, cartilage, and all other connective tissue; particularly collagen type ll (described later)

- *Proteoglycans* (*proteo* for protein; *glycan* for sugar), also referred to as *mucopolysaccharides*... Complex of protein and polysaccharides (*poly* for many, *saccharides* for another type of sugar); found in maturing chondrocytes of growing antlers;[4] characteristic of bone and cartilage of vertebrates; important for elasticity of joints; basic structural building block of joint cartilage

- *Chondroitin sulfate*...Dominant glycosaminoglycan (see below); major component of proteoglycans, building block of cartilage (present between joints); helps to rebuild degenerating cartilage; found in most animal connective tissues and in high concentrations in velvet antler

- *Glucosamine sulfate*...Component of chondroitin sulfate; amino sugars (molecules derived from protein and sugar); necessary for connective tissue; absence results in early aging; building block of proteoglycans; yield is sixfold greater in tip and upper sections than in middle and base sections of antler,[5] found in lesser quantities in velvet antler

- *Glycosaminoglycans* (GAGs)...Polysaccharide chains that give proteoglycans their unique properties; lubricates joints; important regulatory roles[6]

- *Keratan sulfate* (not to be confused with keratin)... Another GAG; component of proteoglycan; functions in the assembly of the collagen network[7,8]

- *Hyaluronic acid*...Core or "spine" of proteoglycans found in extracellular cartilage matrix (extracellular: outside cell; matrix: substance in which things are embedded); present in all sections of antler[9]

- *Dermatan*...GAG found mostly in skin but also in blood vessels, tendons, heart valves, and pulmonary connective tissue.

- *Growth hormones and growth factors*...Elevated levels of insulin-like growth factor (IGF-I) found in blood of deer during antler growth; other growth factors present include TGF, FGF8, BMP4, NT3; contributes to therapeutic value for humans

- *Nucleotides* (RNA and DNA)...Hypoxanthine and uridene, which may produce anti-aging effects

- *Prostaglandins*...Naturally occurring antiinflammatory agents; effective in a dose-dependent manner; helps regulate lipid metabolism

- *Polyamines*: spermine and putrescine...RNA stimulants

  ~ spermine, found in human sperm and in ribosomes; involved in nucleic acid packaging; plays key role in control of DNA replication

  ~ putrescine, amine associated with putrefying tissue; associates strongly with DNA; suggested as growth factor for mammalian cells

- *Gangliosides*...Promote memory and learning function; important for velvet antler quality; considered by some to be the origin of biological activity of velvet antler[10,11]

- Also identified: unknown *68-amino acid peptide* having antiinflammatory effect, plus a unique growth factor speculated to promote bone healing

In a nutshell, here's how a few of these important substances in velvet antler relate to each other:

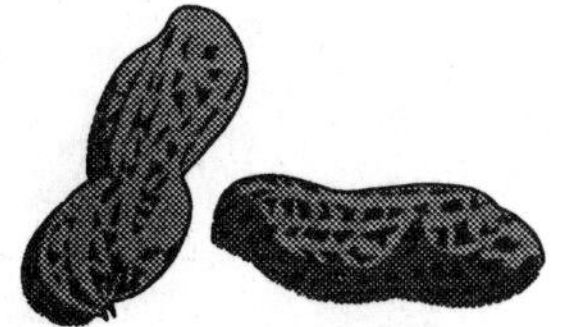

Most of the carbohydrate in velvet antler is proteoglycan, which is a combination of protein and carbohydrate. The carbohydrate portion consists primarily of glycosaminoglycans, of which chondroitin sulfate is by far the predominant constituent.

Dear Antler,

My poor little dog Morgan (a mostly cocker spaniel) can no longer walk, let alone run, on his own. The vet says it's arthritis. Any suggestions ?

Signed: Morgan's Master

Dear Morgan's Master: Dogs don't hesitate to share their fleas with us and we don't hesitate to share our arthritis with them. Does your dog eat table scraps? Does anyone else in your family have arthritis?

Michael and Theresa King had a similar problem with their dog, Prince James. His Royal Highness became a paraplegic, confined to a wheelchair for six months. After giving James velvet antler, he used his back legs independently and even went for walks on his own, just like the other canines in the neighborhood.

And by the way, dogs and humans are not the only mammals afflicted with arthritis.

Good luck. We feel confident that Morgan will be his old self soon.

Chapter 6

What's Special About What's In Velvet Antler?

Let's find out more about the ingredients in velvet antler so that we can have a better understanding of why this product has had such an influence on health for millennia.

Collagen

Collagen has a long history of use other than nutritional. The word collagen itself stems from *kolla*, meaning *glue*, and *gennan*, meaning *to produce*. Yes, collagen produces glue, which continues to be used in large volumes even in today's world of polymerized, manufactured everything. Biologically, it is conjectured that the word came about because collagen has a glue-like effect in your body: It's the "glue" that holds your cartilage matrix together.

But our interest here mainly concerns the ability of collagen to give cartilage its *elastic* quality, and how the long collagen fibers with the proteoglycan molecules assemble to form your cartilage matrix or network.

Cartilage comprises the bulk of the developing antler, but as noted earlier, as the antler approaches maturity, the collagen content of the cartilage matrix decreases and is replaced by bone. You can see why the time of "harvest" is critical to its quality.

Chondrocytes are the cartilage cells that help to manufacture the proteoglycans. They include chondroitin sulfate and other glycosaminoglycans. The nutrients required for these actions reach the chondrocytes through synovial fluid rather than through capillaries carrying blood. This is a very significant fact, and it will be explored later.

Most of the collagen found in velvet antler, sometimes referred to as *collagen type II,* is similar to the kind found in ears, embryonic skeletons, the surfaces of arteries, trachea, larynx, and sides of ribs.[1]

> *Both osteoarthritis and rheumatoid arthritis are associated with the loss of the ability to synthesize or maintain collagen type II.*

When cartilage tissues in your body begin to degenerate, chondrocytes manufacture collagen type I. But collagen type I is not used to produce elastic cartilage, and in fact can cause a depletion of collagen type II.[2] Collagen type II has been useful in reducing the autoimmune reaction (explained later) that causes the inflammation of rheumatoid arthritis. It does this by assisting in the manufacture of immune cells that reduce the inflammation.[3] One of the difficulties in using collagen type II as a treatment protocol by itself is that it is not easily accessible, and therefore very costly.

Most of the collagen in velvet antler is collagen type II.[4]

Although collagen type II is abundant in velvet antler (as with the cartilage matrix of most vertebrates), *type I* is also present.[5] One popular product comprised of *hydrolyzed collagen* is made of type I. Several studies show the effectiveness of hydrolyzed collagen in reducing pain and stiffness,[6] restoration of cartilage,[7] reduction in susceptibility to lumbago,[8] improved general mobility,[9] and benefit to knee and finger joints.[10] Because it is hydrolyzed, this particular collagen type I product is absorbed readily. Collagen type II, however, has the greatest interaction with the proteoglycans.

Cells responsible for growing the antler are also rich in glycogen, making them more like embryonic cells. The presence of mature collagen fibrils (or fine threads) within these glycogen "antlerogenic" cells may reflect the unusually high demand for collagen fibrils during the period of rapid antler growth.[11,12] Glycogen serves as a very efficient energy storage system.

Velvet collagen has been demonstrated to be a healing agent when applied as a topical skin treatment.

Road Map to a Proteoglycan

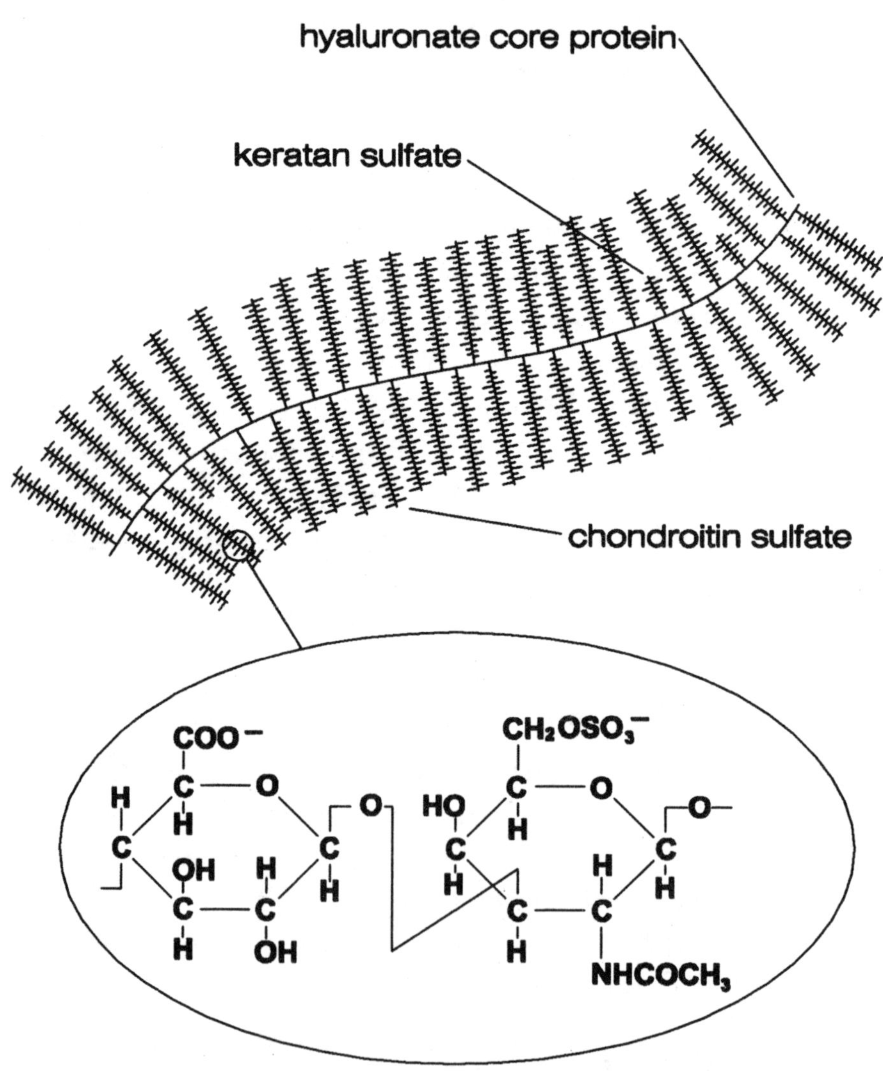

Close-up of the repeating disaccharide unit of a glycosaminoglycan

FIGURE 2

FIGURE 2

ROAD MAP TO A PROTEOGLYCAN

The proteoglycan in articular cartilage can be thought of as a two-sided comb with about 140 teeth. The total molecular weight is around 2 million daltons, more than 100,000 times as heavy as a single water molecule.

The core protein or central backbone is a polypeptide chain of amino acids. Each "bristle" is a glycosaminoglycan (or GAG). Most of the GAGs are chondroitin sulfate, with some keratan sulfate as well.

Each GAG is itself a long comb-like structure, composed of repeating sets of disaccharide units. These disaccharides have negatively charged appendages that repel each other and give the entire molecule its structural and water-absorbing properties. Note how the presence of a shorter keratan sulfate allows the core protein to bend.

Glucosamine sulfate is a basic building block of these disaccharide units.

Proteoglycans

Proteoglycans, along with collagen, form the matrix that gives the cartilage in your joints its special mechanical properties. The ability of these extremely long molecules to absorb and release water is critical to your joint's resiliency. The distribution of electrical charge on glycoaminoglycans, as will be explained, is also an essential feature of proteoglycans that makes this absorption and release of water possible.

Proteoglycans are necessary to allow chondrocytes to control calcium accumulation at the sites where the actual transformation into bone occurs. Recall that *chondro* as a prefix means *relating to cartilage*, so *chondrocytes* are cartilage cells. We know, for example, that the development of long bones in children and adolescents is dependent on the process just described. Because of their rapid growth and regular replacement, plus their easy accessibility, antlers are considered a useful model for the study of cartilage and bone in humans.[13]

In osteoarthritis, the loss of proteoglycans results in damage to the cartilage surface and eventual failure of the collagenous matrix. It can even cause the exposure of underlying bone. Treatments suggested for osteoarthritis that recognize the relationship of proteoglycans to cartilage failure are called *chondroprotective* — a word you may already have seen in the popular press, and one your doctor may have started using.

Glycosaminoglycans (GAGs)

Glycosaminoglycan is a big word for an important molecule. (We appreciate the abbreviation, and will refer to glycosaminoglycans as GAGs from now on.) As indicated, GAGs are a major component of proteoglycans, important because the character of cartilage, as well as the process of converting cartilage to bone, require proteoglycans.

The level of GAGs in velvet antler is a good index of its potency against arthritis.

Procedures for turning a GAG into a useful nutritional supplement can be evaluated by this metric. But keep in mind that isolating these GAG chemicals is second best. They are used as a marker to suggest that other substances — the importance of which may or may not yet be sufficiently known — are also likely to be present.

Chondroitin Sulfate

Chondroitin sulfate is a major constituent of cartilage and is rich in sulfur. The good news is that it appears to be at least partially absorbed after oral intake, and it is an effective antiinflammatory agent.[14] Several clinical studies have demonstrated its *chondroprotective* efficacy in osteoarthritis involving the hip, knee and finger joints.[15]

Chondroitin sulfate is the most common GAG in velvet antler.

Although studies show wide distribution throughout the antler, there are greater concentrations of chondroitin sulfate at the tip and upper sections.[16] The rate of growth of the antler is fastest at the tips — as much as two centimeters per day in some species.[17] The Chinese view about distinct antler sections having different values is confirmed by the fact that different parts of velvet contain varying amounts or formations of the same substance.[18,19]

Growth Hormone

Growth hormones have an *anabolic* effect. They cause tissue to grow, and cause stored energy (fat or sugar) to be consumed. "Anabolic steroid" is a term popularly recognized for this class of hormones, especially in the context of artificial bodybuilding and enhancement of strength and endurance. Anabolic hormones work in opposition to the class of hormones that are *catabolic*, the hormones that cause tissue to break down. (This is an endocrinological dichotomy that is surprisingly consistent with the dichotomy of yang and yin of Chinese medicine.)

Insulin, the hormone released by the pancreas to help metabolize sugar, is *anabolic*, making it possible to build new tissue.

Growth factors are required to control and stimulate the fast growth of the antler. The presence of *multiple growth factors* in the growing velvet is important for antler regulation.[20] It's also important for us: It makes velvet antler so unqiue as a supplement.

Growth factors consist of relatively small proteins (or peptides) which stimulate nuclear DNA to create new proteins. There are many different kinds of growth factors — a subject that is generating a great deal of excitement in our current medical community.

A growth factor for nerves has also been identified in velvet antler. The implications here are that we can help regenerate the spinal column and make repairs in the presence of brain injury. We've come a long way since the time we thought we could never influence nerve regeneration!

> *Extracts of velvet antler were found to stimulate the growth of nerve fibers and to induce changes that affect DNA synthesis.*

So it is that velvet antler boasts a significant amount of important growth hormones and their precursors.[21] This is extremely significant, because growth hormone begins its inexorable decline at about age twenty. The relatively high levels of insulin-like growth factor (IGF-I) found in velvet antler, along with other related cofactors and growth hormone precursors, explain why velvet antler is proving to be such an important unrefined and natural anti-aging supplement.

IGF-I encourages the absorption of chondroitin sulfate and glucosamine sulfate.

Currently active areas of research include efforts to define the involvement of IGF-I physiology in bone remodeling. *Decline in growth hormones and IGF-I are among the causes of the development of bone disorders.* That's why replacement therapy of these growth factors has been regarded as a method useful to protect against osteoporosis progression — an affliction becoming almost as endemic as arthritis.[22] It is especially effective against osteoporosis in growth-hormone-deficient people.[23] IGF-I is classically tied to growth hormone, and often considered a marker of overall growth hormone status.[24]

Because of the elevated levels of IGF-I in velvet antler during the antler growth cycle, antler products are also conjectured to improve muscular development.[25]

Both growth hormone excess or deficiency can lead to changes in the incidence of osteoarthritis.[26] That's one reason you want your growth hormones to be produced by your own body. The best supplementation strategy is to provide your system with the precursors or raw materials so that your body wisdom can then keep things in check. Velvet antler contains these factors.

Growth hormone and insulin

A receptor is a special part of a cell, usually a protein in the cell membrane. The receptor is "tuned in" to respond to the presence of a particular hormone (or drug or other chemical), and then initiate some process within the cell. It's like a radio receiver that can only receive one station. The signal can be incredibly weak, yet still be amazingly effective: Hormone concentration in the blood, as dilute as a single salt crystal dissolved in a large swimming pool, will have a profound effect on physiological functions. The "radio receiver" of the insulin receptor is unimaginably sensitive.

IGF-I "looks" enough like insulin so that your cells' receivers may be jammed by this growth hormone factor, preventing the "insulin signal" from getting through.

It's as if NBC (the growth hormone) was a radio signal broadcast on the same frequency as CBS (the insulin).

But this particular example of receptor "jamming" is not necessarily undesirable or unnatural.

> *The net effect of insulin-receptor suppression, coupled with the action of growth hormone to release stored fat, encourages cells to use up fat rather than sugar or other carbohydrates, with obvious benefits for both body builders and all of us who watch our weight.*

Growth hormone and immunity

Growth hormone also has an important role in immunity. The real nuts and bolts of immunity take place at the cell membrane level, where specialized sentries (proteins, actually) "float" in the thin fatty membrane, controlling what goes in and what goes out. For at least part of the day, it's critical to maintain a protein-building (anabolic) environment: If you can build protein, you can strengthen your immune system. If your protein has to be used to maintain your blood sugar or other crucial out-of-balance functions, then your immunity will gradually degrade.

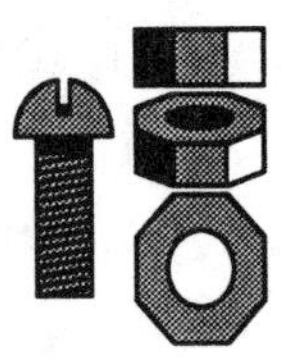

The daily presence of growth hormone for the anabolic effect is enormously important as you age.

Unfortunately, growth hormone production falls off very quickly as you leave your teen years. At age 20 to 23, daytime growth hormone levels begin to drop. By age 30, even the growth hormone release in response to vigorous exercise is significantly reduced. The gym alone won't do it!

Much of the action of growth hormone is carried out through secondary hormones in response to IGF-I and IGF-II. IGF-I promotes bone growth and collagen, while IGF-II stimulates tissue growth. Fortunately the level of IGF-II is not entirely dependent on growth hormone: Even a severe growth hormone deficiency will only result in the IGF-II level dropping to about half the normal value.

So even in an older individual with very low growth hormone production, a natural dietary source of IGF-I, combined with the IGF-II already available, could produce the same anabolic effects found in a much younger individual. This is probably the best way to account for the reported rejuvenating properties and athletic performance enhancement of velvet antler.

Decline in growth hormone and levels of IGF-I during aging may also be a factor in decreased calcification of bone, a condition called osteopenia.[27]

Validation of growth effects

Velvet antler extract was shown to increase growth in mice as early as 1937.[28] Similar results were obtained with chickens and rabbits in the 1970s. In a recent study, it was found that young laboratory rats gained 12 percent more weight than controls after three weeks of dietary supplementation with velvet extract.[29]

This doesn't mean you will gain weight if you use velvet antler as a supplement. The anabolic effect is to burn fat and build tissue. However, the implications for low birth-weight infants, sick children, and the elderly are tremendous.

Why not go straight to growth hormone itself as a supplement? Many studies show that when we ingest hormones orally, our bodies respond by curtailing its own production of that hormone. Another concern is that growth hormone supplementation raises glucose levels. Additional side effects include water retention and "pins-and-needles" pain in extremities. Its use has also been linked to heart disease, and some brands can even produce anti-growth hormone antibodies. Significant morbidity is not unusual. And studies report only marginal functional improvements with direct growth hormone supplementation anyway.

Let your body make its own growth hormone. It knows how to do it best. Your role is to supply the right raw materials (as in velvet antler) to make this happen.[30]

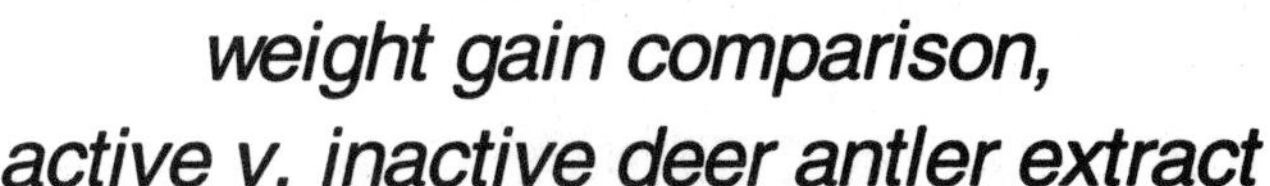

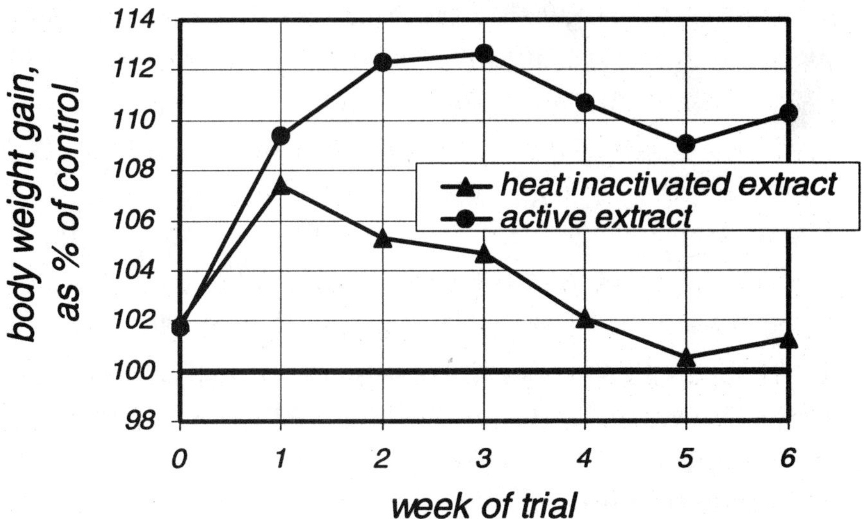

Figure 3

Growth of Test Animals Fed a Velvet Antler Extract

The plot shows the results for the highest dose used in the trial, 100 mg/kg weight. The animals had no ill effects and achieved about a 10-percent weight advantage over controls. Lower doses produced proportionately lower changes in growth rate.

The results also demonstrate that heating the extract eliminated the sustained effect on growth increase, showing the importance of careful processing.

Reference: Suttie JM, Haines SR. "Evaluation of New Zealand Velvet Antler Efficacy and Diagnostic Testing." AgResearch, Invermay Agricultural Centre, Mosgiel, New Zealand, pp32-33.

Prostaglandins

David Horrobin, MD, called our attention to prostaglandins for alleviating PMS symptoms two decades ago.[31] (The first time the average American consumer ever heard the word was when I interviewed Dr. Horrobin on my nutrition radio show in New York City.)

Prostaglandins are produced minute-by-minute from essential fatty acids; they are hormonelike, but tend to be short-lived. In spite of their brief life, they yield a wide range of effects, including control of blood flow to certain organs, smooth muscle management, inflammation restraints, uterine stimulation, and modulation of nerve function. They can even induce sleep.[32]

For our purposes here, it's important to know that some prostaglandins are anabolic agents that stimulate bone formation.[33] It was recently found that osteoblast cells express a very important and newly identified member of the immune system's "super" family.[34] (Recall that osteoblasts are the cells that produce bone.)

Prostaglandins in velvet antler play a role in the reduction of swelling associated with arthritis, injury, infection, and pain, and in suppressing unwanted mineralization. According to recent research, the prostaglandins found in the antler are considered protective against mechanical stress that might interfere with bone formation.[35] Their effects on osteoblasts are just now being investigated and understood. The cholesterol-lowering effects sometimes observed in laboratory animals with the use of velvet antler is explained by the fact that the prostaglandin content also modulates lipid metabolism.[36] This could also clarify the reduced blood clotting shown in animal experiments with the use of velvet antler.[37]

The average American diet contains precursors of the inflammatory type of prostaglandins because of its high content of animal fats, peanuts, and corn oil. Velvet antler contains the precursors for the *antiinflammatory* prostaglandins.

And more...

Other very significant substances in velvet antler include lysophosphatidyl choline, responsible for at least part of its hypotensive activity. Phosphatidyl ethanolamines sphingomyelin, phosphatidyl choline, and the nucleotides hypoxanthine and uriden are potent antiaging factors. Velvet antler's specific polyamines are reported to promote memory and learning function. The 68-amino acid peptide contributes to the antiinflammatory action. The antiulcer effect has been attributed to its polysaccharide content.

Two unique factors stand out when evaluating the constituents of velvet antler.

(1) Velvet antler contains a few substances rarely found in other tissues.

(2) Velvet antler contains some substances in higher quantities than can be found in other tissues.

Now you can see why there is no single active ingredient that defines the special quality of velvet antler. However, we do know that certain trace materials appear to work on their own. Which brings us back to chondroitin sulfate, which brings us to arthritis.

"Honey, I'm home, and I brought you some dinner."

Note: If you happen to be the rare person who is not or does not know an arthritic, we suggest you read the next chapter anyway. It may help to provide insight to many other aspects of your health.

Chondrocytes to Collagen

Chondrocytes are the "living" cartilage cells, as distinct from the extracellular matrix of long collagen fibers and proteoglycans that give cartilage its physical properties. Chondrocytes manufacture the GAGs and assemble and maintain this matrix.

The GAGs include:

- chondroitin sulfate
- keratan sulfate
- hyaluronic acid
- dermatan

Chondroitin sulfate forms the majority of the "teeth" on the large comblike proteoglycan molecule, with keratan sulfate and dermatan in smaller amounts.

Hyaluronic acid forms the spine of the proteoglycan molecule.

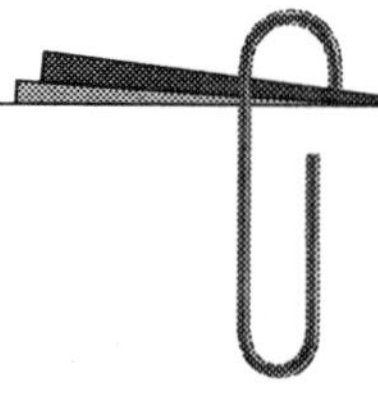

Dear Antler,

All my friends are taking velvet antler and getting rid of their aching knees. Well, my knees are fine. It's my fingers that have me crazed. Please help!

Signed: Digitally Impaired

Dear Digitally Impaired: I've got my finger on some good news for you. A total of 119 patients at the Department of Rheumatology, Ghent University Hospital in Belgium, were included in a scientifically controlled trial to assess the use of chondroitin sulfate in osteoarthritis of finger joints. The result is important since arthritic finger joints can become a serious problem, with pain (you already know that) and functional loss (you already know that, too), showing deformities in time. Treated patients were protected against this erosive evolution. The same velvet antler that helped your friends' knees should help you. Velvet antler is loaded with chondroitin sulfate, plus other synergistic stuff that helps it all work!

Reference: Verbruggen G et al.
Osteoarthritis Cartilage
1998 May 6; Suppl A:37-8.

Chapter 7

Arthritis

If you're talking about arthritis to my neighbor Anne, you're talking to the wrong person. Oh, Anne knows a great deal about the subject. She herself is arthritic, and she goes to the "best" doctor, she reads the "best" books, and she logs on to the "best" sites on the Internet.

I've often wondered who complains more, Anne about her suffering or Anne's family about Anne. Her family doesn't really believe that anyone who takes so many round-the-clock pain killers could have so much round-the-clock pain. I know enough about Anne and her disease to be convinced that Anne really experiences ongoing agony.

Anne does *not* enjoy not being able to comb her hair or butter her toast. It isn't easy to convey to those who enjoy good health what it's like when "everything hurts all the time." Arthritis can affect virtually every part of your body, and in Anne's case, she'll tell you it has.

Nor is it easy to sit by and watch someone you care about suffer — especially when you know *it doesn't have to be that way.*

Anne won't listen to any claims about unconventional therapy. Her doctor told her not to. She trusts her doctor. She has spent enough time in his office for him to share almost everything he knows about arthritis. But whenever he prescribes a new drug, he dispenses hope rather than truth: He doesn't tell Anne that our medical community simply hasn't been able to understand arthritis enough to make it go away. Nor does he tell her that he isn't really all that good at preserving health. *The medicine he knows and practices has nothing better to offer.*

Sadly, Anne is hardly alone. Millions of Americans are physically derailed by arthritis, America's No. 1 crippling disease. According to the Arthritis National Research Foundation, arthritis:

- is progressive
- erodes the physical endurance and pain tolerance of its sufferers
- claims a new victim every thirty-three seconds

Imagine! *Every thirty-three seconds!*

Even more tragic, juvenile arthritis affects an estimated 285,000 children in the United States. For many, it begins when they are very young and follows them like a bad dream into adulthood.

In 2020, an estimated 18.2 percent of the population will suffer from arthritis, up 15 percent since 1995, as reported in *Arthritis and Rheumatism*. And if you think arthritis is a disease of the elderly, you are mistaken. *More than half of arthritis patients are under 65*. Like so many other degenerative diseases of our time, the affliction is taking hold at earlier and earlier ages.

Now the good news: While Anne and her family and millions of Americans are miserable, there are other stories to tell.

~ Joy Beck's hands used to be so bad she couldn't knock on a door without severe pain. Now she could knock a door down.

~ Philip Berne could work on accounting ledgers in his sleep, but he couldn't do it without sleep. He's back on the job, well rested.

~ John Cleave's discomfort became the center of his universe. He couldn't turn over in bed or sit up without help. His knees were swollen. He couldn't feed himself because he couldn't raise his arms. All that is in the past.

~ Corrine Smith said the places it hurt were beyond counting. After a five-year reign of torment, it took Corrine only one month to shed her disability.

~ When Millie McMann sat still for awhile, her first steps were anguish. Today she has complete pain-free range of motion, even after day-long sessions at her computer.

~ Mary Bartlett felt that her biological clock was breaking the sound barrier. But how could she plan to lift a baby when she couldn't lift a book? She's doing just fine now, thank you, with a twin in each arm.

We know it is unlikely that any single nutrient could be responsible for such turnabout results. In fact, almost all these people reported a longtime involvement in taking a handful of isolated nutrients.

So what *did* they do to increase their energy, reduce their aching, restore their mobility, diminish their swelling?

Joy, Philip, John, Corrine, Millie, and Mary are using age-old *velvet antler*. You already know that velvet antler contains antiinflammatory factors, plus many other critical agents beneficial for curtailing a body's response to arthritis.

Controlled and meticulous scientific research is very much in place today to authenticate its success as therapy for the widespread burden of arthritic joint problems. Even the FDA is in agreement:

In 1999, the chondroitin sulfate and collagen type II in velvet antler were scientifically substantiated by research and clinical studies, in compliance with FDA regulations "to support healthy joint structure and function."

This means that velvet antler has received the green light to be marketed as a dietary supplement for the nutritional support of the very body parts that malfunction in the presence of arthritis: *your joints*.

What Arthritis Is

When I lecture and list the benefits of velvet, two areas elicit great enthusiasm from my audiences. The first is its anti-aging properties. The second is arthritis relief, perhaps each for the very same reason:

"Other evils can mend, but age and arthritis get worse every day."

The major divisions of arthritis are osteoarthritis and rheumatoid arthritis. Osteoarthritis, considered a process of aging, is the most common form, afflicting from sixteen to fifty million North Americans — depending on whose statistics you examine. Osteoarthritis is not necessarily what its name suggests. As explained, *osteo* refers to bone, and you probably know that *itis* refers to inflammation. This is something of a misnomer, because osteoarthritis does not always involve inflammation, while many other joint problems do.

Rheumatoid arthritis is an autoimmune disease in which the immune system attacks some of the same joint tissues that are involved in osteoarthritis. White blood cells mistakenly devour healthy cartilage in the joints. Rheumatoid arthritis is a chronic, inflammatory disorder causing stiffness and pain in joints and muscles, usually those of hands and feet, particularly knuckle and toe joints. Joints gradually become inflamed and swollen, leading to destruction of tissue and, in severe cases, deformity.

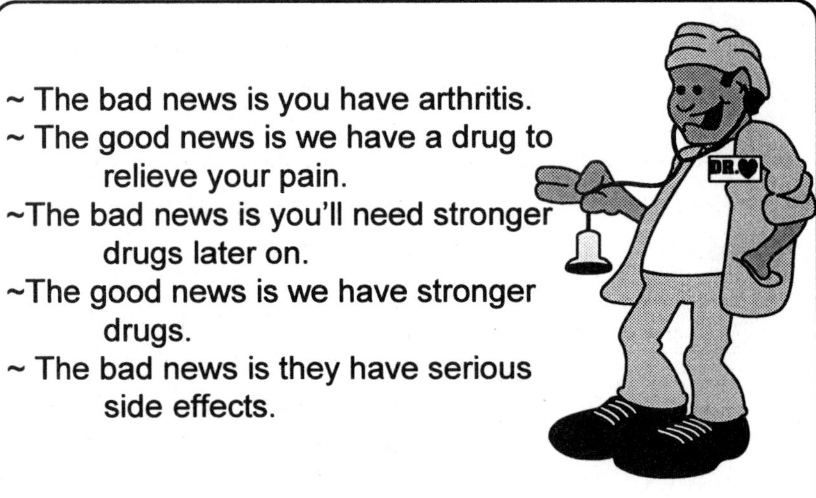

Osteoarthritis is usually age-related, and not genetic, but is affecting more people at a younger and younger age. Rheumatoid arthritis often occurs in young people, with a predominance in women. Genetic propensities may exist, but can be intercepted with lifestyle changes.

Medical Dictionary Definitions

ARTHRITIS: Can be infective, autoimmune, or traumatic in origin. Name stems from Greek word "arthron," meaning joint.

OSTEOARTHRITIS: Noninflammatory degenerative joint disease, characterized by loss of the articular cartilage (which means narrowing of the joint space), hypertrophy of bone at the margins, and changes in the synovial membrane. Pain and stiffness accompany it, particularly after prolonged activity. It is caused by inflammation, breakdown, and eventual loss of the cartilage of the joints.

RHEUMATOID ARTHRITIS: Chronic inflammatory disease in which there is destruction of joints. Considered by some to be an autoimmune disorder in which immune complexes are formed in joints and excite an inflammatory response (complex mediated hypersensitivity). Cell-mediated (type IV) hypersensitivity also occurs and macrophages accumulate. This in turn leads to the destruction of the synovial lining. Can cause inflammation of tissues in other areas of the body (such as the lungs, heart, and eyes). A chronic and progressive course is common with joint deformities.

Source: OMD, On-line Medical Dictionary; Academic Medical Publishing;

Website:http://www.graylab.ac.uk/cgi-bin/omd; Online+Medical+Dictionary

Osteoarthritis

Osteoarthritis is right up there with the major causes of death and disability in women in this country. They are, in order: heart disease, cancer, stroke, fractures, pneumonia, *osteoarthritis*, and cataracts.[1]

Osteoarthritis is often thought of as a disease of "wear and tear" — that is, the material in the joint loses its resiliency and wears away over a lifetime of movement and physical stress. But osteoarthritis has very little to do with wear and tear, and the appearance of this disease does not correlate well with too much exercise or a high physical activity level. In fact, exercise and a physically active lifestyle may have preventive effects, as will be explained.

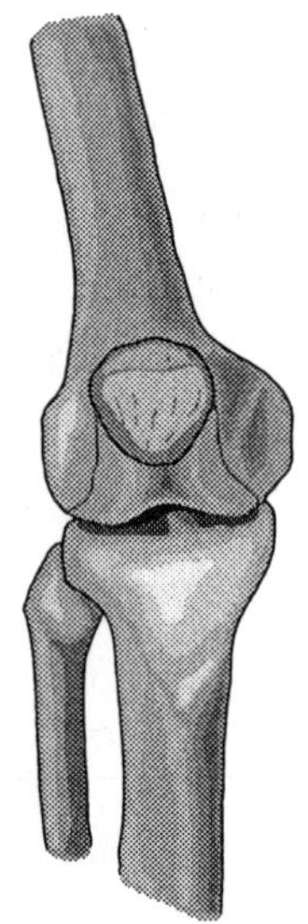

What actually happens in your body to create the condition?

A Little Anatomy

Very few of your bones actually touch each other. At least they shouldn't. A layer of an amazingly strong, slippery, and resilient material between your bones should absorb all the pressure and shock, yet remain almost totally frictionless as your joint moves.

This material is *articular cartilage* — articular because it allows your joint to articulate or bend (creating a natural separation of joints), and it is 65 to 80 percent water. The rest of the cartilage matrix is comprised mostly of collagen and proteoglycans. Recall that collagen is an essential structural building material for many types of body tissue including hair, nails, bone, and skin. In articular cartilage, the collagen is in the form of long, stringy microscopic fibers.

Proteoglycans are interwoven all around the collagen fibers. It's something like crocheting onto a lattice. The special chemical properties of the proteoglycans give the cartilage matrix its unique structural and lubrication properties.

Articular cartilage, or joints, form pads on the ends of the mating bones, and these are immersed in a bath of liquid called synovial fluid. Synovial fluid is transparent, resembling raw egg white. Without this lubricating and insulating fluid, movement would be difficult and painful. The fluid is contained by the synovial membrane, the tissue responsible for producing the nutrients that are transported to the joint tissue itself.

The entire joint is contained in a joint capsule, which includes ligaments, joint fluid, and other types of cartilage for further cushioning of the joint. This tough membrane produces lubrication and maintains the integrity of the joint.

A Typical Joint and the Articular Cartilage Matrix

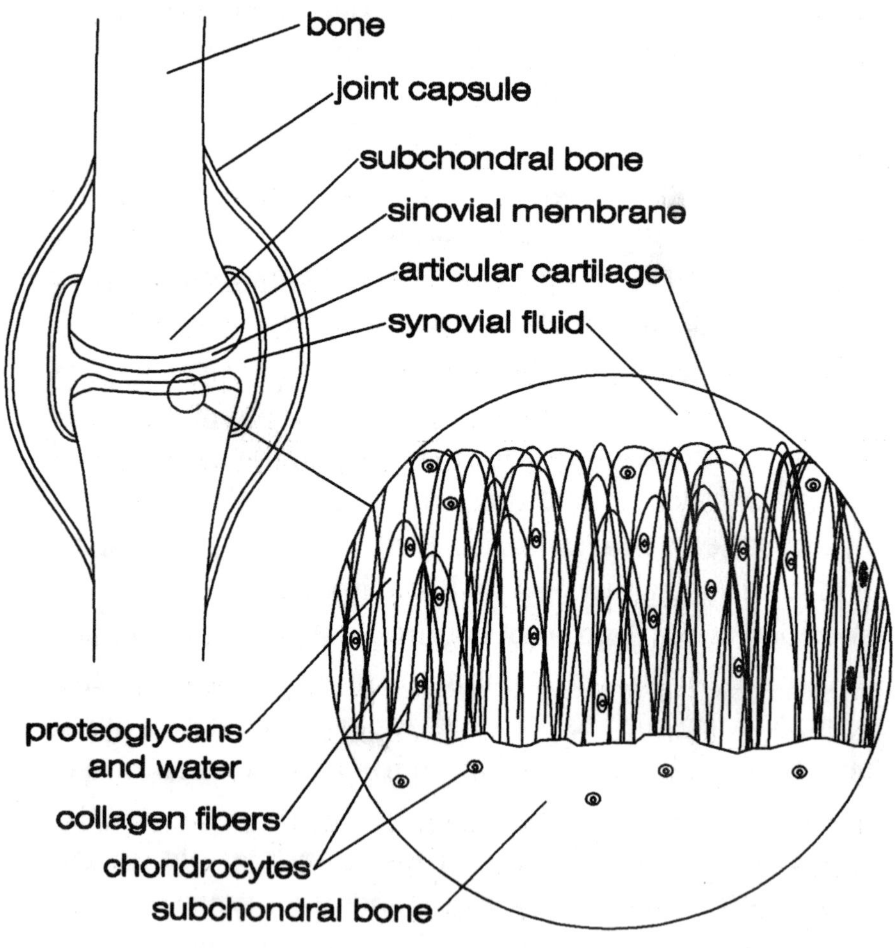

FIGURE 4

A little physiology

In some joints, the articular cartilage must transmit your entire body weight between the ends of the two bones on either side of the joint. In fact, whenever your foot hits the pavement, the sudden impact causes the instantaneous load on your knee joint to be many times greater than your body weight.

Articular cartilage is under far too much pressure to contain a normal system of blood vessels and capillaries. The pressure in a knee joint, for example, would squeeze out the blood from such a system like toothpaste from a tube. But nutrients must still be carried to and from the cells that build and maintain this matrix of collagen and proteoglycans. Instead of blood, the synovial fluid is the medium that carries nutrients in and waste products out.

Unlike your vascular system, there's no heart pumping this fluid around; it relies entirely on the motion of your joints — the alternate squeezing and releasing of the articular cartilage and the changing geometry of the joints to keep the synovial fluid in motion. Synovial fluid enters and exits the articular cartilage almost like water going in and out of a sponge that's continuously being compressed and released.

That's just one reason why exercise can be beneficial.[2] Without a blood supply, it takes longer for things to diffuse in and out, which is why it takes so long to heal cartilage or repair disc problems in the spine. (Discs are mostly cartilage.)

Exercise is the "heart" of your joints. In this case, exercise might even be considered a "nutritional" treatment. This was demonstrated in a study in which researchers noted the effects of weight-bearing exercise on patients with osteoarthritis of the knee. The participants received a thrice-weekly low intensity exercise program for three months. Conclusion: pain levels definitely declined.[3]

> *Without the alternating compression and expansion of the articular cartilage and of the synovial sack itself, nutrients could only diffuse slowly into and out of the areas where they need to go.*

In spite of overwhelming exposure about the importance of exercise and the endless health attributes it offers, only a small minority of Americans do so on a regular basis. And still fewer engage in yoga, yet another helpful stratagem because it helps to stretch the spine.

"When I get the urge to exercise, I lie down until the feeling goes away."

Exercise and Joints

As is so often the case, animal research is far ahead of human research:

~ A study was done to show the effect on articular cartilage and synovial fluid in hamsters because they, too, get osteoarthritis. The exercising hamsters did well, unlike their sedentary relatives. The control group (the sedentary animals) had lower synovial fluid volume.[4]

~ The rapid response of bone and cartilage to mechanical stimulation has been researched extensively in equine athletes, leading to appropriate exercise changes in their training.[5]

~ A small proteoglycan of the cartilage matrix (called decorin because it decorates collagen fibers) was shown to increase in articular cartilage in dogs after long distance running exercises.[6]

A little biochemistry

The nature of articular cartilage is also very specialized and very critical for the proper function of the joint. The key materials are the GAGs. If you could see an enlarged and simplified version of the proteoglycan molecule, you'd see a structure that looks something like a very long comb with teeth on both sides of a central spine. The individual teeth are GAGs. Each of these "teeth" has teeth of its own — actually the negatively charged molecular branches attached to each disaccharide element of the GAGs. (See Road Map, Figure 2, page 56.) And each of these tiny teeth carries a negative electrical charge near its tip, so they all repel each other due to static electrical forces.

This is somewhat the same as the repulsion between similar poles of two magnets. The result is that all the GAGs remain spaced apart, and their design attracts water molecules to fill the spaces between them.

This is how the articular cartilage can stay saturated with water even under the high pressures of load-bearing exercise.

Cartilage, however, dehydrates as we age.

Other important components of articular cartilage are the chondrocytes. They are responsible for manufacturing the collagen and the proteoglycans, and also for assembling and repairing the cartilage matrix.

Remember that these cells do not have access to a blood supply for nutrients and raw materials. Everything they require in order to assemble cartilage has to come from the synovial fluid.

Part of the function performed by the chondrocytes involves destroying old cartilage to make room for new.

When things go wrong

Equilibrium should exist between the production and removal of collagen and proteoglycans in healthy cartilage tissue. But excessive cartilage destruction can damage the joint itself, actually causing the matrix to lose its ability to retain water.

> *The end result is that the cartilage becomes dry and hard, subject to cracking and pitting.*

Some initial damage or change to the cartilage matrix may trigger this process. The number of chondrocytes then increases in an attempt to repair the cartilage, with the result that still more old cartilage is destroyed. For some reason the new cartilage cannot always be made fast enough to keep up.[7] In the analogy of crocheting onto a lattice, it's as though stitches keep getting dropped, and you cannot crochet fast enough to replace the dropped stitches.

Demolition and recreation occurs at a certain rate, but, again, when this balance is upset, we lose more cartilage than we produce. Chondrocytes need to be active in order to keep the cartilage recycling and renewing.

Even if there are plenty of active chondrocytes, other shortages can compromise the cartilage. If there's a shortage of GAGs, the proteoglycans lose their ability to attract water, the joint cannot recover from compression, and elasticity is lost. This reduction in the in-and-out flow of the synovial fluid in turn reduces the nutrient supply to the cells that would normally reconstruct the proteoglycan molecules, further aggravating the problem, *and the vicious cycle begins.* It's like being unable to replace a flat tire on your car because you can't drive to the auto supply store to get a new tire.

In the extreme case, after the joint loses its elasticity and lubricating properties, the articular cartilage itself begins to wear away. Additional bone material sometimes forms in an attempt to make up for the loss of cartilage, leading to uneven surfaces and very rough and painful joint motion — like having a bone spur inside your joint, or stepping on a tack that cannot be removed. Ouch!

The pain originates in the nerves of the sensitive synovial membrane. But this pain is the body's natural and desirable response: It's the signal to stop what you're doing and give the joint a chance to heal. Inflammation can help too, increasing the supply of fluid in an attempt to send nutrients to the chondrocytes in order to restore the lost cartilage. But when you are the one suffering, it's not much consolation to know that these unpleasant effects are really in your best health interest.

Treatment

Drug-based treatment

Anti-pain and antiinflammatory drugs, regardless of the relief they provide, don't address the cause of the problem. Worse, they may interfere with healing.

Therapy for osteoarthritis is presently mostly palliative and is based on pain-suppressing or antiinflammatory agents, from over-the-counter NSAIDs (pronounced en-sayds, the acronym for nonsteroidal antiinflammatory drugs), cortisone-like drugs (steroids), gold salts, and even experimental cytotoxic (cell-killing) drugs.

Simple analgesics (painkillers), however, do not provide enough of an effect to satisfy the needs of many osteoarthritic patients, and currently available antiinflammatory drugs do not have a favorable risk-to-benefit ratio in typical patients.[8] Furthermore, drugs believed to be state of the art only a few years ago already have an antique look.

NSAIDs are by far the most common therapy for arthritis. If you use NSAIDs, such as ibuprofen (Motrin), naproxen (Naprosyn), oxaprozin (Daypro), nabumetone (Relafen), or diclofenac (Voltaren), you should be aware that they cause bleeding from the gastrointestinal tract in almost 25,000 people every year. Although the new Cox 2 inhibitor Celebrex avoids the bleeding problem, other side effects may exist. (See below.)

Some of these drugs interact unfavorably with high blood pressure medicine. New evidence shows that long-term use of NSAIDs can cause liver and kidney damage, and may even accelerate the destructive nature of arthritis. The FDA cautions that patients who are chronically treated with NSAIDs are subject to serious gastrointestinal toxicity, including ulceration and perforation in addition to the bleeding, which can occur at any time — with or without warning symptoms.

Peptic ulcer complications related to use of NSAIDs are among the most common serious adverse drug reactions.[9,10] A host of small bowel manifestations have now been documented with the use of NSAIDs, ranging from obstruction and severe bleeding to a syndrome of increased intestinal permeability and low-grade inflammation with blood and protein loss.[11]

The more you use NSAIDs and the longer you use them, the greater your risk.

And then there are steroids. Steroids are powerful drugs that work fast. By suppressing your immune system response, steroids lessen swelling, soreness, and allergic reactions. In some cases, steroids give your body a chance to heal itself, but in the case of arthritis, it's little more than a temporary fix. Everyone knows by now that steroids are powerful medicines with dangerous side effects. Because they suppress your immune system, they can lower your resistance to infections and even make infections harder to treat. Furthermore, they can cause bone loss.

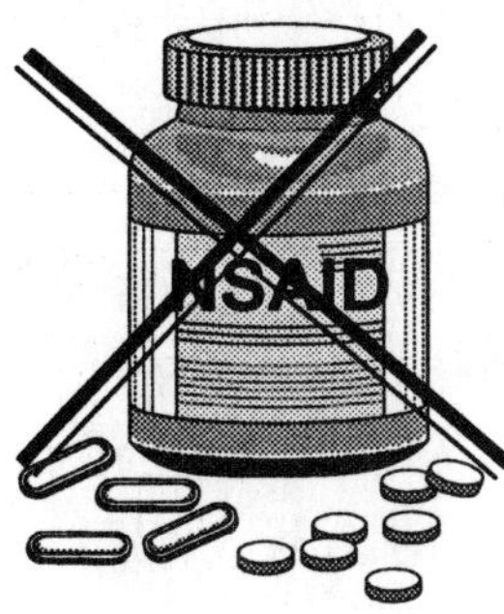

After all that risk, neither NSAIDs nor steroids alter the arthritis process itself. When the drugs fail, surgery is usually the final option: removal of badly inflamed joint synovium, joint realignment, joint reconstruction, tendon repair, joint fusion, or artificial joint replacement.

"Isn't it amazing," said a veterinarian friend of mine recently, "that higher animals have more pharmaceutical ability to produce natural alternatives for healing than our gigantic pharmaceutical industry? Our attempts to manipulate life in the laboratory usually fail."

Caveat: Safety concerns surrounding two new arthritis drugs, Celebrex and Enbrel, were recently cited. Enbrel is associated with many reports of serious infections since its approval in November 1998. And although there were ten fatalities among patients taking Celebrex, the FDA issued a statement indicating that consumers need not worry: Cause of death appeared to be related to other factors. (Monsanto stated there was no causal relationship.)[12]

Nutrient-based treatment

A better approach is to keep your synovial fluid well supplied with GAGs, so that water absorption capability and elasticity are never lost. This can be done with velvet antler and, to a lesser extent, with other animal connective and joint tissue, even meat gristle.

> *One study demonstrated that a regimen of chondroitin sulfate for several weeks at the dose of 1200 milligrams a day lowers prescriptions of NSAIDs, which can be completely avoided in nearly half the cases.*[13]

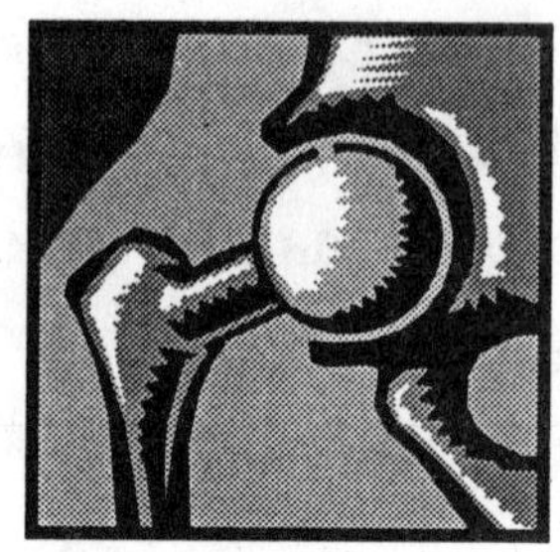

At the Department of Rheumatology, University Hospital, Liege, Belgium, it was shown that glucosamine sulfate has the effect of stimulating chondrocytes to manufacture significantly more proteoglycans — one of the raw materials needed by the chondrocytes, and possibly the "rate limiting" ingredient.[14] Rate limiting refers to the situation where the shortage of only one of many ingredients determines how fast the process can proceed. For example, if you are making concrete and only have a limited amount of sand, it doesn't matter how much cement, water, and gravel you have available. You can only make concrete as fast as the sand arrives. Current theory is that the amount of proteoglycans produced may be contingent on how much glucosamine sulfate is available.

Chondroitin sulfate is a much larger molecule that includes the charged part of the "comb teeth" of a proteoglycan. This is the molecular structure responsible for the incredible water-absorbing properties of articular cartilage.

> *A single proteoglycan molecule may contain 10,000 chondroitin sulfate chains.[15]*

Chondroitin sulfate and glucosamine sulfate, when taken in supplemental form, appear to work synergistically, although this is still a debatable issue. Some practitioners claim good results using one and not the other, some claim best results using both together. The success of the combination is no surprise. In 1999, a sixteen-week trial was conducted, involving glucosamine (1,500 mg/day), chondroitin sulfate (1,200 mg/day), and manganese ascorbate (228 mg/day) in degenerative joint disease of the knee or low back. The study was randomized, double-blind, placebo-controlled, and crossover. You can't get more scientific than that! Result: The combination therapy relieved symptoms of osteoarthritis of the knee.[16]

Bill Walton, famous basketball player, had recurrent foot fractures. He was discovered to have severe manganese deficiency. For years we have been objecting to America's passion for taking large amounts of calcium. *Large amounts of calcium interfere with manganese absorption.* Half of your body's manganese is found in your bones, and it is essential for the formation of the mucopolysaccharides (the proteoglycans) needed for healthy joint membranes.[17] But manganese in supplemental form, taken long-term, has its own shortcomings. We constantly return to square one: *Get your nutrients from whole foods or whole-food-type supplements.*

If the mixture of these powerful materials — the chondroitin sulfate, the glucosamine sulfate, and the manganese ascorbate — was so effective, you can understand the favorable results reported with the use of velvet antler. Velvet contains a huge cluster of additional nutrients. Some physicians will recommend the use of adjunct chondroitin sulfate for their patients who are badly compromised. But remember, the velvet growth factors and other constituents of the velvet antler help to enhance the effectiveness of chondroitin sulfate.[18]

A sufficient number of newer short-term studies with both glucosamine and chondroitin sulfates have been done, suggesting efficacy equal to that seen in the treatment of osteoarthritis using NSAIDs. Much as we prefer the use of whole-food type supplements, it goes without saying that these isolated substances are far superior to the drugs.

Two May 1999 meta-analyses reports reviewed clinical trials of glucosamine and chondroitin for osteoarthritis. (Meta-analysis refers to a method of combining the results of independent studies and synthesizing summaries.) One study tested for treatment of hip or knee osteoarthritis. The authors concluded that these two agents showed substantial benefit. The other study compared glucosamine with placebo, and glucosamine was always superior to the "empty pill." Pooled data demonstrated at least 50 percent improvement in the study variables in the chondroitin-treated group.[19]

Glucosamine is rapidly developing a position as therapy for wound healing and gastrointestinal disorders as well as osteoarthritis. Although recognized for a great many years, the association of gastrointestinal disorders and arthritis has been looked on as an unexplained oddity. Could a variety of diseases be due to a common biochemical defect?[20] Is that why so many people report that serious problems, in addition to arthritis, are relieved with the use of velvet antler?

Hyaluronic acid:

Synovial production of hyaluronic acid, which is essential for the lubricating and shock-absorbing properties of synovial fluid, may contribute to beneficial effects. Clinical and veterinary studies show that injections of hyaluronic acid produce rapid pain relief and improved mobility in osteoarthritis. Hyaluronic acid not only has antiinflammatory and analgesic properties, it promotes anabolic behavior in chondrocytes.

Since hyaluronic acid is decreased in synovial fluid in osteoarthritis, reversing this abnormality provides rapid benefit, and in the longer term aids the repair of damaged cartilage.[21] What better way to accomplish this than with the use of a product containing *all* of these substances working synergistically and safely to accomplish these goals?

This encourages the more significant factor: Other nutrients and pathways play a role as well.

> Example of biological interdependence: proteoglycans are stimulated by the addition of concentrations of combinations of growth factors.[22]

Oxidative damage

Joint degeneration may also be caused in part by oxidative damage. Oxidative damage is the same mechanism that makes over-bleached socks fragile, turns old rubber bands brittle, causes fats and oils to go rancid, and can impair the proper function of virtually every cell membrane in your body. Oxidized fats can be particularly damaging because one molecular fragment, charged by oxidation, can cause many more molecules to oxidize in a kind of molecular chain reaction.

The diet for healthy joints should minimize exposure to these dangerous charged particles, called free radicals. But they are provided in abundance by burned, oxidized, rancid, or over-processed fats and oils.

"It's going to rain. I feel it in her bones."

The Real Cause of Osteoarthritis

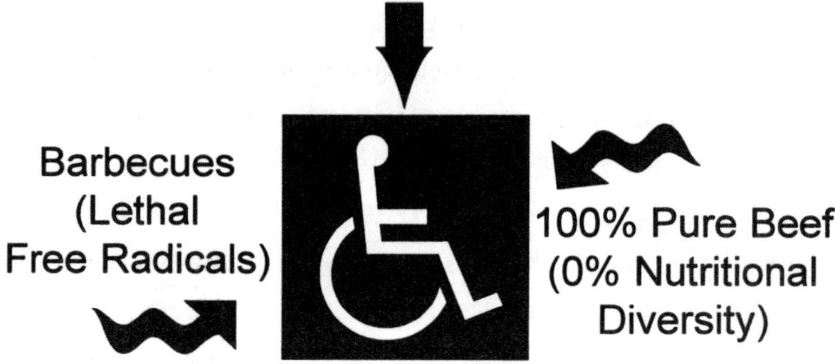

What we're really saying is that osteoarthritis is caused by the combination of lack of exercise, poor nutrition, and especially the failure of our modern diet to include more parts of the animals we eat.

A sedentary lifestyle starves the cells in your joints by not circulating enough fluid to bring in the nutrients needed to keep joint tissue in good repair. Poor nutrition, especially high levels of oxidizing contaminants and low levels of natural antioxidants, accelerate the degeneration of tissue and make repair more difficult. The lack of dietary trace materials from animal connective tissue, especially chondroitin sulfate, deprives joints of an ample supply of the most important raw materials it needs to keep itself in good repair.

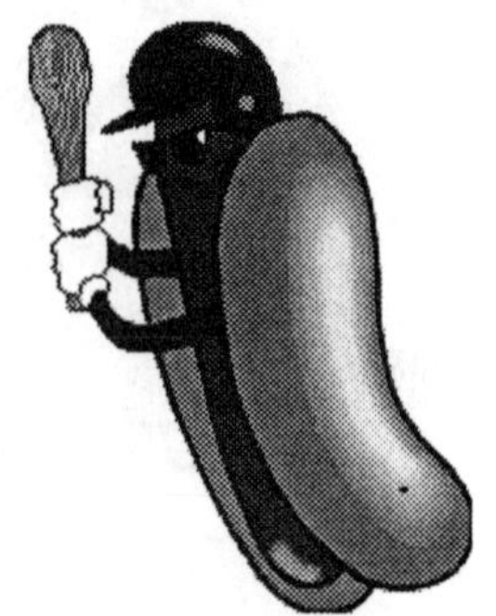

What you can do about it:

All three of these factors can be corrected. But from a real-world, practical application point of view, there's one discrepancy: How can we eat animal connective tissue without also exposing ourselves to deadly burned and rancid saturated fat and the free radicals we must avoid for optimal health?

In theory, the answer is to eat these animal parts raw — the kind of food our bodies evolved to thrive on. Even if we could do it safely, eating raw gristle and bone is not considered a viable option. Certainly not by us!

We are left, then, with specialized foods that concentrate the factors that are missing from our deficient diets. Velvet antler seems to be custom-tailored to correct a number of critical deficiencies when used as a food supplement.

A disturbance in one organ is unlikely to be localized in that organ alone, but instead corresponds to some element of disorder in *all of you*. Examples abound: A diabetic suffers from more than just pancreatic disturbances; women who have menopausal symptoms have other things going askew in addition to difficulties with ovarian function; etc., etc.

> *Velvet antler is a ready-made package that helps to heal all of you.*

Laboratory validation of velvet antler for osteoarthritis

- As early as 1974 pantocrin, described earlier, was shown to have antiinflammatory activity.[23]
- Researchers demonstrated potent antiinflammatory effects from antler extract in 1996.[24]
- A recent study in New Zealand demonstrated anti-inflammatory effectiveness in laboratory mice.[25]

Clinical validation — comparing chondroitin sulfate with an NSAID Or: Healing Vs Nonhealing

A convincing clinical trial involved 146 patients with osteoarthritis of the knee. Some of the subjects were given the conventional drug *diclofenac sodium* (150 mg/day), while others were given chondroitin sulfate (1200 mg/day).

The trial first confirmed that the standard drug works. The diclofenac group experienced rapid pain reduction. But the pain quickly returned when the treatment stopped. In the chondroitin sulfate group, pain reduction was achieved at a slower rate, but symptoms did not fully return until three months after the supplementation ended. The graphs (see Figures 5 and 6, pages 102 and 103) compare the relief from osteoarthritis symptoms provided by the two treatments. The dotted lines continue after the treatment ended. The researcher's report follows:

> "Diclofenac, a well-known NSAID used extensively in joint pathology, produced prompt and potent antiinflammatory capability during the administration period. However, when treatment was suspended, progressive regression toward the previous state confirmed that NSAIDs are not able to modify the natural course of the disease.
>
> "On the other hand, the intake of chondroitin sulfate was associated with a relatively slow variation of the symptoms (modifications were evident from day thirty of the treatment), later presenting results comparable to those of diclofenac. The benefits, however, lasted longer; even after the suspension of treatment. Symptoms tended to reappear only toward the sixth (and final) month of the observation period."[26]

The implication is that chondroitin sulfate is different, and is actually doing something that arrests or even reverses the course of osteoarthritis.

Even if you don't "have" osteoarthritis, you can be sure some measurable change in the shape of your cartilage has occurred by the time you turn thirty-five. If you're over fifty-five, your doctor would be surprised if you had no symptoms of arthritis. By the time you reach your eighth decade (your 70s), you have a 90 percent chance of having some degree of the disease. It makes perfect sense to include a velvet deer antler supplement as a standard component for your joint-health regimen.

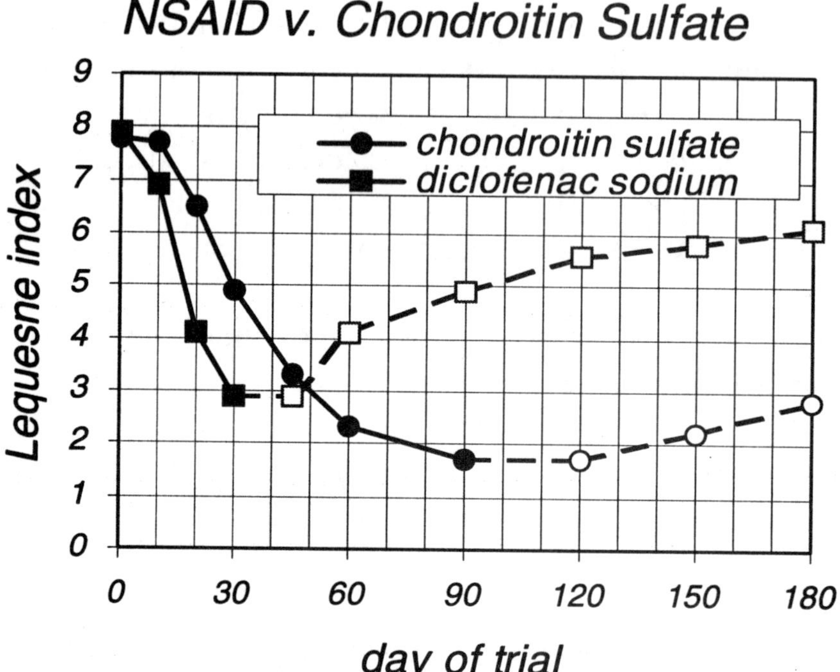

FIGURE 5

Comparing Effects of Chondroitin Sulfate with a Nonsteroidal Antiinflammatory Drug

The Lequesne Index is a standard method for evaluating the severity of osteoarthritis of the hip and knee.

Chondroitin sulfate, considered to be much safer to use for a much longer period of time, takes longer to work but has more long-lasting effects. The drug, diclofenac sodium, was administered for one month at 150 mg/day, then replaced by placebo for the remaining five months. The chondroitin sulfate was given for the first two months at 1200 mg/day, then replaced with placebo.

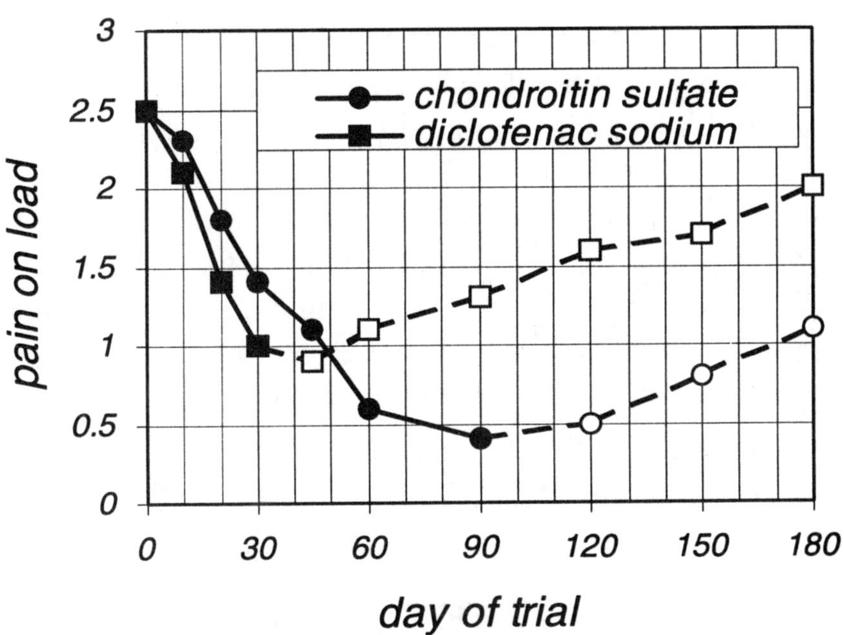

FIGURE 6

The same study, showing pain measured on a 4-point scale.

0 = no pain
3 = severe pain

The researchers suggest that chondroitin sulfate may actually be addressing the cause of the disease, rather than simply masking the symptoms.

Reference: Morreale, et al. "Comparison of the antiinflammatory efficacy of chondroitin sulfate and diclofenac sodium in patients with knee osteoarthritis. *Journal of Rheumatology* 1996;23:8.

Rheumatoid Arthritis

Developing a therapeutic strategy for rheumatoid arthritis has been considered a difficult and much debated task by our medical community.

Unlike osteoarthritis, which progresses steadily over time, rheumatoid arthritis is a condition that waxes and wanes. One may suffer either a single attack or several episodes, possibly leading to increasing disability. Rheumatoid arthritis is also associated with damage to lungs, heart, nerves, and eyes. It's seen mostly in those between the ages of 40 and 60, but it can also affect children and teenagers. Three times more women than men are afflicted. It is considered an autoimmune problem because the defense mechanisms of your immune system attack your joint tissues as if they were the enemy — a warlike reaction to normal body components, sometimes triggered by bacterial or viral infection.

In rheumatoid arthritis, the synovial membranes become inflamed, and immune cells attack both cartilage and bone. Fortunately, the immune response can be selectively inhibited by certain cytokines, which are "good-guy" immune molecules, cells released to beneficially affect the activity of other cells. But the helpful immune response has to be triggered to promote secretion of these inhibiting factors.[27]

Collagen type II has been used with some success in both experimental animal trials and in a human study against some types of rheumatoid arthritis.[28] It appears to stimulate T-cells to make more of the necessary cytokines.[29] The process can be thought of as a kind of gradual conditioning — with long-term oral administration of collagen type II eventually desensitizing the immune system to the substance, so that the autoimmune response diminishes.

Called "oral tolerance," this concept is also being used as a wondrous new treatment for multiple sclerosis and uveitis (inflammation of the iris and surrounding structure), in addition to rheumatoid arthritis.[30,31] By reintroducing collagen type II from an outside source, the immune system is somehow "trained" to break off its attack. Reminder: *Velvet contains collagen type II.*

The presence of anabolic growth factors in the inflamed synovium may have a major impact on destruction of the articular cartilage in rheumatoid arthritis. It is suggested that therapy should include attempts at reduction of *cartilage* destruction. We know that cytokines are found in the inflamed synovia, causing problems. Yet local administration of cytokines, which enhances their content, *almost fully prevents cartilage damage.*[32] More puzzles for the scientists to unravel.

Clinical validation:

In one study, sixty patients were divided into collagen and placebo groups. The group given collagen type II for three months reported significant reductions in joint swelling and pain, and a few patients even claimed complete remission. Patients receiving placebo experienced no reduction of their rheumatoid arthritis symptoms.[33]

Collagen type II may also have a significant role in the treatment of juvenile rheumatoid arthritis. After three months of treatment, 8 of 10 patients using oral collagen type II experienced reduced pain, swelling, and stiffness, along with increased grip strength and ambulatory endurance.[34]

Recall that velvet antler contains hyaluronic acid, which contains glucosamine and forms the core of complex proteoglycan found in the cartilage matrix. A 1999 study showed that rheumatoid arthritis patients treated with hyaluronate improved, compared to a control group. The viscosity (thickening) of the synovial fluid increased.

> *The researchers agreed that hyaluronate altered the properties of synovial fluid, demonstrating benefit for patients with rheumatoid arthritis.*[35]

Traditional treatment for rheumatoid arthritis includes advice to rest. However, as with osteoarthritis, exercise induces changes in circulating immune function that would appear helpful in regulating the inflammation. And there is evidence that rheumatoid arthritic patients can tolerate a program of regular moderate aerobic exercise, enhancing physical performance without exacerbating the disease process.[36]

Velvet and the FDA

The average perception is that osteoarthritis is common, and that it is debilitating, costly, incurable, and, in many cases, resistant to treatment.[37] That view is changing, with the blessings of the United States government agency, the FDA.

Many popular (and ultimately quite effective) natural remedies cannot legally be sold in the United States under specific claims that describe what they do. Part of the problem in achieving acceptance by the FDA is the cost involved in conducting the required trials. The absence of a patentable proprietary substance makes investing in such trials a very poor risk. A natural product found in humans, in an animal, or even in a plant cannot be patented without some alteration.

But, as indicated earlier, in 1999 velvet antler was scientifically substantiated by research and clinical studies, in compliance with FDA regulations "to support healthy joint structure and function." Velvet antler has achieved a status that many other valuable nutritional supplements do not have, mainly because of its content of chondroitin sulfate and collagen.

As you now know, the clinical applications of velvet antler do not stop with arthritis or joint disorders.

Dear Antler,

I'm madly in love with this woman, but she's noisy. That is, her body makes strange noises. She tells me she can't control the creeky sounds, that her doctor says they're joint noises. Do you think that's possible?

Signed, Bothered

Dear Bothered,

The answer to your question can be found in the following abstract of a journal article.

The signs and symptoms of osteoarthritis are common complaints seen in patients suffering with chronic temporomandibular disorders (TMD), internal derangement with a diagnosis of osteoarthritis. With or without the complaints of pain and swelling, joint noises are bothersome and annoying to both the patient and at times, to those seated close to the patient during mealtime. In fact, many patients are driven to seek care by family members because of their TMJ noises.

Recent reports support the use of chondroitin and glucosamine sulfates for decreased joint noises.

Reference: Shankland WE 2nd. "The effects of glucosamine and chondroitin sulfate on osteoarthritis of the TMJ:a preliminary report of 50 patients." *Cranio* 1998 Oct;16(4):230-5.

Chapter 8

Other Conditions Helped with Antler

Because of his enthusiasm for velvet antler, Michael Rosenbaum, MD, enjoys sharing stories about his patients who have had success using it. And when Dr. Rosenbaum describes patient histories, it's more than anecdotal. He measures the blood chemistry to validate the results.

He told us about one patient who plopped himself down in his office with the very familiar stance of fatigue and depression. "I just have no 'oomph' anymore, doc," said this successful businessman. His construction company was doing just fine, but something was missing, and he didn't want to go the pharmaceutical route. He had been to several other "nutrition-oriented" physicians, and had swallowed lots of vitamin tablets. He even had nutrients infused directly into his bloodstream. Dr. Rosenbaum's testing revealed a low testosterone count.

Since the patient stated that he had tried everything else, Dr. Rosenbaum suggested velvet antler. The patient came back a few weeks later, beaming. After a very short time on a daily dose of 300 milligrams of velvet antler, he experienced a miraculous change, described as a sense of overwhelming power. “I never felt better,” he said. His testosterone count now reflected his *joie de vivre*.

Another patient suffering from “guitarist thumb” overcame that problem within a few weeks with the use of antler. Other problems that resolved with velvet antler follow.

Athletic Performance

In some ways athletic performance is a more interesting gauge than disease recovery or prevention because it does not begin with the premise of a physiological dysfunction. Furthermore, athletic performance depends on a number of different physiological systems working at optimum efficiency. When evaluating a nutritional product for use as a systemic tonic, athletic performance data is relevant even for the non-athlete. In addition, results are usually more immediate, rather than at the expected “slow pace of natural.”

Pantocrin, discussed earlier, was observed in the late 1960s to have a positive effect on the endurance of laboratory animals.[1] Based on these findings, trials in Russia included one study in which subjects were given either pantocrin or rantarin (reindeer antler), and the results were then compared with those of controls. Athletes in the antler extract groups outperformed the controls by far.[2]

Another study showed a significant increase in running speed, with time over a 3,000-meter course dropping from 14:48 to 14:04. Although it's not clear if the trial was controlled, the results as reported suggest that a single dose of velvet antler extract was responsible for this improvement, and that further reductions in time were observed after twelve days of use. The benefit was equally distributed across all ability levels.

Motivated by such an impressive information base, the Russian Bodybuilding Federation picked up the research. Dr. Arkady Koltun added velvet antler to his studies of anabolic agents and their effects on strength, endurance, and muscle composition. It was suggested that the elevated performance levels were due to a velvet antler-induced increase in the ability of muscle tissue to recover from physical or biochemical stress following exertion.[3]

Dr. Arkady's research demonstrated that velvet antler was beneficial to both muscular and nervous system function.

We mentioned earlier that pantocrin enables test animals to recover quickly from whiplash-like injuries. This effect is believed to be due to increases in glycolysis, a necessary process in the maintenance of healthy nerve tissue. Glycolysis is a process whereby your body breaks down certain carbohydrate molecules (usually glucose) to energy. (The suffix *lysis* means dissolution or disintegration.) It's the first step in glucose breakdown used in anaerobic metabolism.

In a placebo-controlled trial conducted in New Zealand, the participants were found to experience a slight increase in weight lifting ability after ten weeks of treatment.

> *Researchers noted that velvet antler induced red blood cell formation and stimulated increased muscle mass.*

Combined with the antiinflammatory action and reported lactic acid removal efficiency, these effects help to enhance muscle composition, endurance, and recovery time.[4]

Lactic acid is produced as a result of exercise, often causing muscle aches and pain. Efficient removal of lactic acid assists in preventing many undesirable effects, including its deleterious actions on central nervous system tissue.[5]

Testosterone Increase

A nine-week study with Edmonton, Canada police recruits with velvet elk antler supplementation resulted in significantly increased testosterone levels.

Elk antler was chosen because of its protein content and the relative stability of these proteins during processing. The increased testosterone stimulation and levels noted in the results were theorized to be due to the antler's rich source of particular amino acids considered responsible for stimulating testosterone release from certain cells in the testes — encouraged, in turn, by velvet antler-induced signals from hormones. The cells involved are *leydig* cells, assumed to furnish the internal secretion of the testes. The hormones that inspired their additional activity are *luteinizing*, which control sex hormones in both men and women.

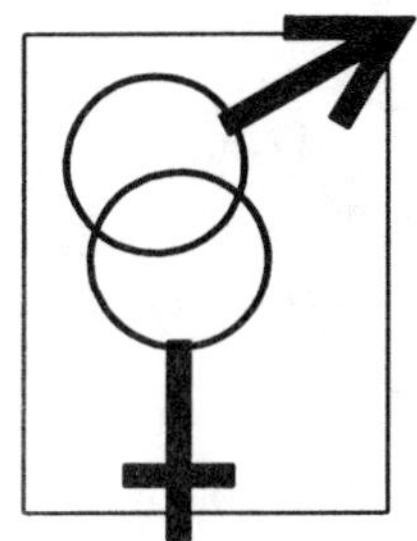

Other theories of the mode of action have been suggested, but there is little question that velvet elk antler has a significant androgenic, or masculine, effect.[6] (Just what new police recruits need today — more testosterone!)

Testosterone is currently being used for both men and women to increase libido. As an isolated supplement, however, it is fraught with side effects.

TESTOSTERONE, WOMEN, AND LIBIDO

A new study (June 23, 1999) shows that postmenopausal women who receive testosterone in addition to estrogen replacement therapy experience increases in muscle mass and decreases in fat mass compared with women who use estrogen alone.[7] Don't get too excited: It also lowers "good-guy" cholesterol. The researchers noted that the effect on lipids as they pertain to cardiovascular risk are not yet clear, but several practitioners suggest that women taking testosterone are indeed subject to heart disease.

In the natural context of the velvet antler, taken in recommended amounts, the side effects experienced by the testosterone content are nonexistent. That's the power of an effective *natural* adaptogen.

Studies like this demonstrate that it's possible to manipulate body composition. But let's do it without side effects.

It has also been shown that the extracts rantarin and pantocrin have androgenic effects, increasing the production of testosterone and its metabolites. In this respect, velvet antler may function in a similar way to the supplement androstenedione (which became a household word at the end of the 1998 baseball season thanks to Mark McGwire). Androstenedione is a steroid precursor to testosterone and other androgens, produced naturally by the adrenal glands and gonads. It is converted to testosterone in the liver, ovaries, and testicles. While no long-term studies on the performance-enhancement use of androstenedione exist, many users believe that it helps develop muscle mass and reduce recovery time following injury or stress.[8]

One-third of the women in this country have had a hysterectomy. It's interesting to note that supplemental testosterone enhances some aspects of sexual function in surgically menopausal women. Sexual pleasure and orgasm improve significantly overall, as does the frequency of any kind of sexual activity. But there is a safety issue because most preparations have not been fully tested, and there's a real potential for harm.[9] Once again, this is a score for velvet antler, which provides the hormone in a more balanced, adaptogenic manner.

It's also interesting to note that most older males with osteoporosis have low normal or below normal testosterone.

Testosterone is said to help with many things including anaerobic increases in muscle (lean body mass); decreases in body fat in men (especially the dangerous abdominal spare tire related to heart disease); increases in vitality, stamina, endurance, libido, erections, and the ability to overcome erectile dysfunction. (Senator Dole, pay attention. Drugs have side effects.)

Immunity

Scientific validation of the effectiveness of particular products showing effects assigned to our immune system can be hard to produce. But some studies do exist supporting this benefit for velvet antler.

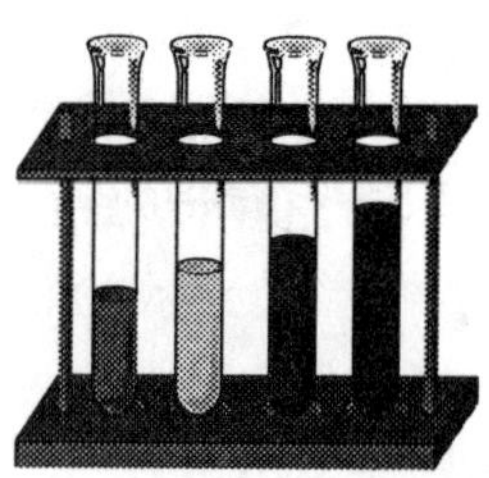

Pantocrin has been shown to stimulate the action of phagocytes, the cells that engulf and destroy bacteria, in both normal and immune-deficient test animals.[10]

The dosage showing these results was 0.5 to 2 mg/kg. That's roughly equivalent to a 150-pound person requiring 34 to 136 milligrams daily.

Monocytes are among the more important protective white blood cells circulating in your blood. They are critical to the immune function of your lymph, spleen, bone marrow, and connective tissue.

Experiments with laboratory animals show that monocyte counts increase with the inclusion of velvet antler extracts as a dietary supplement.[11]

When eight New Zealand antler extracts were evaluated, it was determined that those prepared from freeze-dried antlers harvested at days 60 or 85 after "button drop" had significant immune stimulant activity. No mode of action was proposed, although the researchers suggest that the response is caused by cytokines in the antlers, involving antibody stimulation. Concentration ranging from 500 mg/ml to 15 mg/ml were studied, and it was found that all extracts, even those at the low end of the scale tested, had a measurable effect. That statement is so significant, it bears repeating:

It was found that all extracts, even those at the low end of the scale tested, had measurable immune effects.

We associate velvet antler's beneficial actions on immune function as the result of growth hormone and its precursors. But GAGs may also produce an immune-enhancing result. Their ability to interact with human interferon and the effects of these interactions on biologic activity was analyzed. The data suggest important regulatory roles for GAGs on the activity of cytokines of the immune system.[12]

Cancer

Some therapeutic properties of velvet appear to be similar to those of cartilage. Shark cartilage in particular has received a lot of attention in the last few years for its apparent anticancer properties, and velvet may share the same mode of action.

For several decades there's been sporadic interest in using cartilage for the treatment of certain classes of degenerative diseases, notably osteoarthritis and cancer. In the early nineties the potential of this substance in cancer therapy was considered enormous, although since then enthusiasm has faded a bit. However, new interest in using cartilage in the treatment of arthritis and related diseases has again come to the forefront, partly as a result of observed secondary effects during cancer therapy.

Cartilage not only holds your bones together, but it also holds your muscles in place and shapes your skin. Although technically it's living tissue, the metabolic activity level of mature cartilage is extremely low. It seemed unlikely that this relatively inert tissue that appears to do nothing more than provide certain mechanical properties to joints and limbs would play any role at all in systemic health problems.

But the inactivity of cartilage is also the reason for its importance. When normal tissue propagates, blood vessels grow with them. In most tissue, a capillary is never more than a few cells away. But in cartilage the formation of blood vessels is suppressed.

The very nature of cancer is runaway cell propagation. Cancerous cells grow and multiply out of control, stealing nutrients and crowding out other cells until the function of the affected organ is compromised. Along with this very rapid tissue growth is the formation of the infrastructure to support the new tissue in the form of additions to the circulatory system. It's like building new freeways to support new suburban sprawl.

Cartilage, however, appears to contain its own control mechanism to prevent development of new blood vessels. And these substances seem to be able to do this selectively. That is, they only suppress blood vessel formation when the growth rate is too fast. In the suburban sprawl analogy, this is like the city planner refusing to grant permits for the new roads. Development becomes economically infeasible, and the "cancer" of unbridled suburban expansion is forced to stop.

This is the primary mode of action of cartilage against cancer. When substances from cartilage are present, formation of new blood vessels is suppressed in fast-growing cancerous cells. They don't receive the nutrients (the new roads) they need to survive, and the cancerous propagation is constrained.

In addition to this effect, two other main anticancer mechanisms appear to be at work. An aggressive cancer needs to destroy some of the surrounding tissue to make room for itself. It is believed that this is accomplished by means of specific chemicals, and cartilage appears to reduce their activity.

The modern medical use of cartilage began with Dr. John Prudden of Columbia University Hospital in 1957. Prudden had considerable success using bovine cartilage as an antiinflammatory agent, with healing rather than destructive side effects.[13] Quoting from a cartilage update report by biochemist Stephen Levine, PhD, and chemist Arnold Takemoto,[14] Prudden "presents impressive data on the use of bovine tracheal cartilage in areas on the reversal of cortisone-induced wound healing, antiinflammatory effects in a broad array of autoimmune disease, rheumatoid arthritis, osteoarthritis, psoriasis, reversal of dermal thickening and loss of elasticity of scleroderma."[15]

It would be reasonable to conclude that anything that inhibits blood vessels would also inhibit healing. But cartilage seems to contain a kind of elusive chemical intelligence of its own. There are reports of increased healthy tissue growth surrounding cancerous areas in patients using cartilage as supplemental treatment.

Dr. Prudden turned his attention to cancer treatment, and shark cartilage has been associated with the fringe of alternative cancer therapies ever since.

The Shark and the Elk

Shark cartilage is economical to harvest, but the special attention to the shark as a cartilage source probably relates to the fact that the shark has an all-cartilaginous skeleton. This is a very old configuration for a vertebrate species. Sharks have been around for about 400 million years (compare this to dinosaurs, which became extinct only 65 million years ago), long predating animals and other fish with true bones.

The cervids are a much younger species than either the shark or the dinosaur, but the antler contains a very intense application of cartilaginous growth control, which is the key to its success for human supplementation. When we know more about the actual mechanisms of cartilage metabolism, we'll be able to use it with more precision. Meanwhile, since the whole velvet antler works, there's no need to understand everything going on under the hood in order to use it effectively.

"You've got to eat all that cartilage, so your joints and bones will look good in a museum some day."

The third way in which velvet antler might find broad application against cancer is in mitigating the negative effects of conventional anticancer drugs.[16] Velvet antler increases the effectiveness of the chemotherapy drug given to test animals, and also reduces kidney damage.

The mode of action has not been determined, but the results are consistent with the traditional use of velvet antler as a tonic that rejuvenates, strengthens, and corrects. And of course velvet antler enhances macrophage functions and immunity, critical in cancer care.

Other Enhancements

In China, there is widespread belief that velvet antler improves mental capacity. In the 1596 document referred to earlier, it was listed as improving vision and hearing. It is suggested that certain lipids can in some way influence conduction of nerve impulses by influencing electrical conditions. This is just one of many avenues yet to be explored. The more information we get, the easier it will be for people to make informed decisions as to whether velvet antler will be useful for them.

~~~

After all these years of selective eating and supplement use, velvet antler is one of the few products that has made a difference for our family members.
~~~

Letter from Stan, Mike's Agent

"I am the executive vice president of a series of pet stores. My dog, co-star and best friend Mike is not stiff anymore and now walks up and down the stairs by himself, thanks to elk velvet antler.

"Mike is a 10 ½-year-old boxer who was rescued from a humane society. He had a tough life, and was diagnosed with spinalosis. He has arthritis and a very poor immune system. Over the last few years, his ailments have gotten worse. He had no energy, was very stiff, and I had to lift him up and down stairs.

"I'm happy to report that Mike is now doing great. He climbs stairs by himself, and has more energy and is definitely a happier, healthier dog. He's the star of a TV show for dogs, and even "writes" a column for a newspaper. Velvet antler has added years to his career."

Dear Antler,

I don't have arthritis, or any signs of it. In fact I'm in great shape — unlike so many of my friends, all of whom are taking velvet antler supplements. Should I be taking them, too? I worry about spiralling costs of health care.

Sincerely, Well, But Worried

Dear Worried Well: As a member of the Worried Well, you have plenty of company.

But, are you eating your meat fresh-killed, raw, and gnawing on the bones and gristle? If not, then you're not getting the kind of nutrition your body evolved to thrive on. A velvet antler supplement can help to fill that gap.

Every day, we get a day older, and that means less efficiency in all kinds of metabolism. And yesterday's tomorrow is already here. Consider velvet antler an insurance policy. Continue to stay well, without the worry.

Chapter 9

Velvet Antler as a Supplement

The Antler Business Today

North American ranchers raise approximately 110,000 elk, the largest of the deer family. The average bull elk will produce 15 to 20 pounds of antler each year, for as long as 15 years. Historically, the velvet antler harvested by North American farmers has been exported to Asian countries. But as the natural food and dietary supplement market has expanded in the United States, farmers have turned their attention to the domestic market.[1]

The handwriting has been on the wall: In the June 1999 issue of *Natural Pharmacy*, velvet antler was described as one of the "hot supplements for 2000 and beyond!"

As stated earlier, the North American elk (or wapiti) and the red deer are the two species now cultivated in North America for antler production. Again, no significant differences have been found in the composition of the velvet antlers from these two breeds.[2]

New Zealand is the world's major producer and exporter of velvet antler, supplying the voracious Korean market. Their stock is similar to the red deer and elk imported from Europe in the mid-nineteenth century. But antler farming as an industry did not begin in New Zealand until 1970. China and Russia are also current velvet antler producers, each with their long tradition of antler farming to supply their own domestic demand.

Are all velvet antler products created equal?

> *The species that provides the antler does not seem to be critical for therapeutic effectiveness.*

As noted earlier, velvet can be significantly different depending on exactly what part of the antler it comes from and at what time in the antler's growth cycle it was harvested. Large variations in composition of the final product also depend on processing, storage, and the method of application (capsules, tea, powder, etc.).

The evaluation of an velvet antler product depends to some extent on the reasons for using it. For arthritis, chondroitin sulfate appears to be the closest thing to a single active ingredient that has been identified to have curative effects. As explained, however, and as is often the case with nutritional supplements, reducing an effective adaptogenic food substance down to an active ingredient may be counterproductive.

We believe among the crucial elements of velvet antler is its content of growth factors. To the best of our knowledge, only two other commercially available substances contain significant amounts, and these are (1) an extract of the nucleus of chlorella algae, and (2) colostrum.

Absorption

Can chondroitin sulfate and some of the other important cofactors in velvet antler be absorbed orally and retain their bioactivity? Recent research indicates that despite the relative large size of the chondroitin sulfate molecule, the answer is yes.

The absorption of GAGs administered by oral route is a controversial question, arising from the difficult-to-accept notion that molecules with high molecular mass may pass through gastric and intestinal mucosa."[3] But while absorption rates of GAGs vary, the oral administration of chondroitin sulfate has been demonstrated to be significant.[4]

Absorption rates of chondroitin sulfate were investigated in test animals and in healthy volunteers. A rapid absorption of oral chondroitin sulfate was observed in animals and in humans when the it was dissolved in water. Lower and delayed absorption occurred when it was administered in gastroresistant capsules.

Even if chondroitin sulfate is considered the primary active ingredient of antler, the presence of glucosamine sulfate might be critical because it seems to act further "upstream" in the process of building healthy cartilage. The fact that these two substances are found together supports the notion that the whole natural velvet antler product, properly handled, will continue to outperform any one of its constituents used in isolation.

Here's an interesting example: Despite a significantly lower zinc content in breast milk compared to formula, the zinc in breast milk is more bioavailable — that is, more readily assimilated.[5] The breast-fed infants show higher zinc levels than the babies who are formula fed with higher amounts of zinc supplementation. This is just one model of increased bioavailability of a nutrient when ingested in the context of a whole and natural substance, as nature intended. It is conjectured that, among other constituents, the presence of growth factors in antler facilitates the absorption of the chondroitin sulfate and/or its assimilation into renewed cartilage.

Is It Safe?

The only known adverse side effect of consuming velvet antler is an upset stomach when taken in very high doses, a difficulty reported to disappear when the dose is discontinued. (And of course there should be no reason to consume large quantities.) Beyond that, no adverse effects have been noted. As a natural tissue that has been consumed for thousands of years, the safety of this substance has had more than adequate time to become well accepted. Because they are so modest by comparison, the doses available to North Americans do not initiate any ill effects.

My friend Ping Hou, who grew up in China, tells me about the velvet soup her mother made for the family. It was a wonderful concoction, based on a hunk of the actual velvet thrown into the pot. It became the *soupe du jour* for anyone in the family who was getting over an illness. Ping described unpleasant reactions from this extremely potent elixir for herself and her recuperating siblings: These symptoms were amazingly similar to those we experience when we are on strict detoxification programs. But the benefits overreached, by far, those of our familiar clean-up-detox consommés.

My Korean produce vendor told me his mother dispensed the water in which she boiled an antler segment to the younger children. At least one research paper reports that such water has been used successfully for curing a series of illnesses.[6] (My mother created an amazing green thumb simply by feeding her plants the water in which she steamed vegetables.)

On a trip to Malaysia, I was changing planes in Hong Kong, with time to spare. I went to a lunch counter where the special of the day was *knuckle bone soup*, with rice and an egg roll. Recall that the only significant food source of chondroitin sulfate is animal cartilage.

Selecting Your Product

Chondroitin sulfate comprises about 90 percent of the total GAGs in velvet antler.[7] As we have noted, other cofactors are undoubtedly important, and we should not fall into the trap of putting all our eggs in one biochemical basket. That's why we believe it is still best to use a *food product* that contains high amounts of chondroitin sulfate, rather than a pure chondroitin sulfate supplement in isolation, even if combined with glucosamine sulfate. Holistic paradigms, rather than reductionist attempts, have almost always proved to be best for attaining the goal of optimal health. And we don't say that lightly. Nutrient labeling does not improve nutritional quality! If a higher quantity of chondroitin sulfate is necessary to do the job, at the very least it should be taken along with velvet antler.

> Caveat: If you do go the "isolate" route, and you are sulfur-sensitive, look for N-acytyl glucosamine, rather than the sulfite complex.

We have seen that velvet antler cannot really be viewed as a single nutritional supplement. Again — evidence suggests that time of harvest, part of antler used, and processing methods all play a role.

Unfortunately, today's consumers are not yet in a position to fine-tune their choice of velvet antler products with these variables in mind. Even the producers of velvet antler supplements are just beginning to grapple with these subtleties, although future practitioners will in all probability be able to pick and choose from a matrix of products based on known attributes. This is already done to some extent in traditional Chinese and Korean practices when a particular part of the antler is specified. We predict that as the dawn of the new millennium unfolds, it will bring with it a greater melding of this age-old wisdom and the assemblage of insights brought in from corners of biologic, high-tech science.

Back to the Caldron — or the Stew Pot

If you observe a predator eat its prey, you will rarely ever find any leftovers. Even predators eating the same animals that we eat leave nothing but perhaps the largest bones and maybe a bit of tail.

It is not unreasonable to conjecture that humans, too, evolved in a nutritional environment in which just about all of anything they killed was eaten, worn, or slept on. Velvet antlers, it's safe to assume, have been consumed by humans for many millennia before their medicinal properties were written up in the silk scrolls found in that ancient Chinese tomb. And it's only in the last century or so that humans have had the collective poor sense to end the common use of organ meats as a routine part of their cuisine.

Few of us are willing to return to a "whole animal" diet. But velvet antler, as we have seen, offers a practical way to restore some of the health benefits we really never should have lost. North America is rediscovering the healing power of a special substance, marking the return to an ancient form of health maintenance that had been taken for granted for thousands of years. We can only wonder what we might be missing by leaving eye of newt and toe of frog out of our modern diets.

~~~

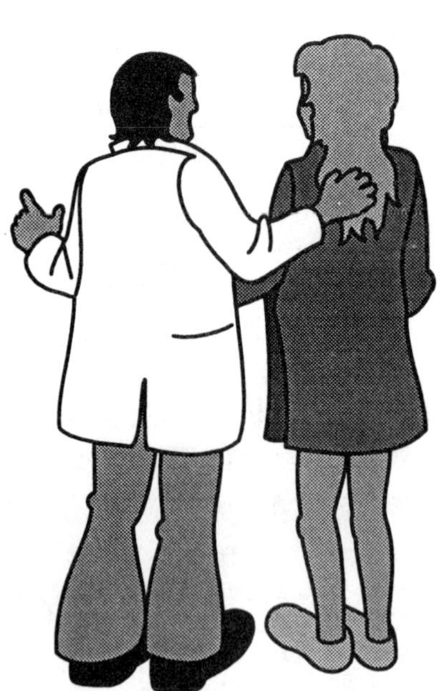

"What's a joint like that doing in a nice girl like you?"
~~~

A Letter from David Wadman

"A bad bout of the flu interfered with my cycle training, but I caught up quickly, thanks to elk velvet antler. (I'm on a cycling team.) My most significant gain has been high intensity performance, especially for hill climbing.

"After three weeks of distance training, I can push through a six-hour ride without too much difficulty. Even our team physician confirmed that I was at the same level as the riders who had been training longer.

"Thyroid-stimulating hormone is an indicator of whether an athlete has been using growth hormones or other restricted substances. My level was within normal range, one of the factors reported to be influenced by velvet antler.

"When I test myself by not taking the velvet, I find I don't recover from training and racing as quickly. When I'm on the velvet, no matter how long and heavy I train, my muscles heal enough to work them again the very next day. My doctor actually asked me if I was taking steroids because I've gained so much mass in such a short period of time.

"In addition, a knee problem that had once stopped me from jogging because of intense pain and stiffness has completely disappeared now that I'm taking elk velvet antler."

Dear Antler,

Up and down! Up and down! I've been on every diet, and when I stop, I gain more weight than I lost. Help!

Signed, Yo-Yo Annie

Dear Yo-Yo Annie: Welcome to the Club. If you ever find the solution, let us all know.

Several thoughts, though:

~ Growth hormone interacts with fat cells to regulate appetite and energy expenditure.

~ Growth hormone secretion, either spontaneous or evoked by provocative stimuli, is markedly blunted in obesity.

~ Obesity is associated with suppressed growth hormone secretion and an unfavorable lipoprotein pattern.

Velvet antler works toward helping to alleviate these problems!

References:

Hormone Research 1999 May51(2):78.
Journal of Endocrinology 1999 Jun;161(3):511.
Metabolism 1999 Apr;48(4):525.
*International Journal of Obesity and Related Diseases*1999 Mar;23(3):260.

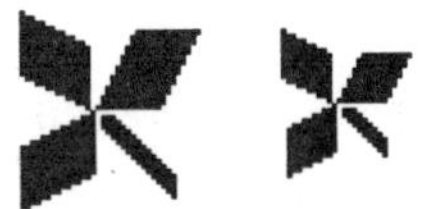

Grandma's Recipe for Bone Soup

Veal joints (knuckles) or young chicken bones, or beef neck , or any young cancellous (latticelike) bones

1 cup barley
2 to 3 quarts water
green vegetables in season
(the more the better)
seasonings to taste

Cook bones and barley in water. Bring to boil and simmer over low heat ½ hour.

Nutrition Tip: No better soup for your aching joints and bones!

APPENDIX A

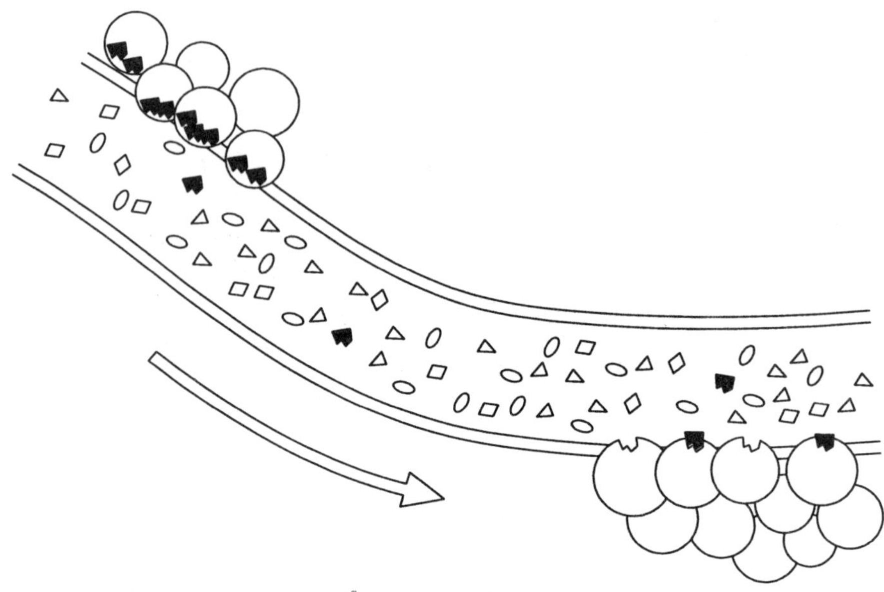

HORMONES:
ONLY A SMALL AMOUNT HAS A
MAJOR EFFECT

An extremely small concentration of a hormone or a hormonelike factor can affect tissue at a remote location. The circles at upper left represent cells in a hormone-producing gland, or those taken orally. Hormones or hormonelike substances are represented by the black particles. These cells enter the bloodstream and will only exit when encountering a matching receptor, as represented by the circles at lower right. Other hormones or molecules are not affected by this receptor — they just don't "fit."

APPENDIX B

You may want to consider a few other food-type supplements. Among our favorites:

~ Probiotics. If digestive functions are impaired, nutrients from the best diet in the world will suffer from compromised absorption. The "friendly" bacteria of probiotics help to restore your ability to resist disease, too often altered by antibiotics, stress, and dietary indiscretions.

~ Green-food mixes. Chlorella and a combination of different sprouted grain grasses are among our favorites. These foods provide a storehouse of nutrients and ideal biological ratios — to make up for the vegetables you forgot to eat today.

~ Colostrum (a newborn's first meal). The most critical components of colostrum are those that offer immediate passive protection by fighting infection. Colostrum overflows with *antibodies* in the form of *immunoglobulins* — complicated molecules specially configured to bind or "stick" to specific *antigens* in bacteria, viruses, fungi, and certain chemical toxins, facilitating their destruction and removal by white blood cells or other components of your immune system.

~ Cytolog. The ability of very small doses of "infopeptides" to turn on powerful antiviral, antibacterial, and antiprotozoal immune functions is very impressive. Cytolog has two major benefits: A return to wellness from an adverse health condition (from lupus to multiple sclerosis) and freedom from general lapses in good health (such as colds and flu).

~ Lactoferrin. Involved in iron metabolism and biochemical processes in lymphocytes, lactoferrin impacts on bacterial growth. Research indicates success in lung cancer and reduction in pain during surgery, plus other benefits.

Beet crystals, garlic, and mushroom mixes, plus vitamin C, can also help to make a difference.

GLOSSARY

Adaptogen Substance, usually natural, having no specific function until needed.

Anabolism Creation; process of building new tissue; opposite of catabolism.

Articular cartilage Material covering bone ends where they meet in a joint; capable of absorbing and releasing water critical to joint's resiliency.

Bone Density Volume of calcium and other minerals within the bone tissue.

Button drop Part of antler remaining after most of antler is removed; sheds at time antler would have been naturally released had it been left intact.

Calcify To make or become bony.

Cartilage Connective tissue dominated by extracellular matrix containing collagen type II and large amounts of proteoglycan, particularly chondroitin sulphate.

Catabolism Destructive metabolic process by which organisms convert substances into excreted compounds.

Chondroblast Embryonic cartilage-producing cell.

Chondrocyte Cell that forms cartilage.

Chondroitin sulfate Glycosaminoglycan that helps attract fluid to proteoglycan molecules; building block of cartilage (between joints); helps rebuild degenerating cartilage.

Chondroprotective Therapy or substance protecting cartilage from damage.

Collagen Insoluble protein substance of the fibers of skin, tendon, bone, cartilage, and all other connective tissue.

Collagen type II Most predominant form of collagen; reduced in arthritic conditions; acts as "skeleton" for proteoglycans; helps to hold cartilage together.

Cytokine Small proteins or biological factors released by cells having specific cell-cell interaction, communication, and behavior of other cells. Term tends to be used as a convenient generic shorthand for important immune molecules.

Decorin Small proteoglycan of the extracellular matrix, so called because it decorates collagen fibers.

GAGs Commonly used abbreviation for glycosaminoglycans.

Gangliosides Origin of biological activity of velvet antler.

Glucosamine sulfate Limiting factor that determines how many proteoglycan molecules are formed in cartilage. The greater the amount, the greater the number of proteoglycans.

Glycolosis Process whereby body breaks down certain carbohydrate molecules (usually glucose) to energy.

Glycosaminoglycans (GAGs) Important proteins in cartilage that help to bind water in the cartilage matrix.

Growth factor Biological substance produced by body to control growth, division, and maturation of blood cells by bone marrow. Regulates division and proliferation of cells.

Growth hormones Hormones with anabolic effects, causing tissue to grow and stored energy (fat or sugar) to be consumed.

Hyaluronic acid Glycosaminoglycan forming core of complex proteoglycan aggregates found in extracellular matrix.

IGF 1; IGF 2 Insulin-like growth factors I and II; polypeptides with similarity to insulin. Capable of same biological responses. There are two types of insulin-like growth factor receptors on cell surfaces, one of which resembles the insulin receptor.

Immunity Protection against infectious disease conferred either by the immune response generated by immunization or previous infection or by other nonimmunologic factors.

Insulin Polypeptide hormone secreted by cells of the pancreas in response to high blood sugar levels; induces hypoglycemia. Diabetes mellitus I is caused by defective secretion of insulin.

Joints Complex units holding bones close enough to make movement possible; helps bones slide gently over each other.

Keratan sulphate Proteoglycan; functions in the assembly of the collagen network.

Lactic acid Produced as a result of exercise; can cause muscle ache and pain.

Linolenic acid Significant essential fatty acid; required in higher amounts by humans than other fatty acids.

Matrix Loose meshwork within which cells are embedded.

Monocytes White blood cells; involved in first line of immune defense and in inflammatory process; precursors to mácrophages.

NSAID Nonsteroidal antiinflammatory drug recommended for alleviation of pain and inflammation reduction.

Osteoarthritis Noninflammatory joint disease, characterized by degeneration of articular cartilage.

Osteoblast Cell that gives rise to bone or aids in growth and development of teeth and bones.

Osteoclast Cells that break down bone.

Osteoporosis Disease characterized by decrease in bone mass and bone density, plus increased risk of fracture.

Pantocrin Deer antler extract.

Pedicle Permanent pedestal-like projections from deer's skull, from which antlers grow.

Phospholipids Lipids (fats) containing one or more phosphate groups, of great importance for structure and function of cell membranes; most abundant of membrane lipids, although not stored in large amounts in the system.

Prostaglandins Group of components derived from fatty acids having variety of important roles in regulating cellular activities, especially in inflammatory responses

Proteoglycans Large group of biologically active compounds synthesized from unsaturated fatty acids having a wide assortment of biological effects, some of which are: fluid balance, blood flow, gastrointestinal function, and neurotransmission.

Rantarin Deer antler extract.

Receptor Cell component that combines with a drug, hormone, or chemical to alter function of that cell..

Resorption Breakdown and assimilation of bone through action of osteoclasts.

Rheumatoid arthritis (RA) Characterized by chronic joint inflammation and infiltration by cells from blood, especially activated T cells and macrophages, together with formation of new blood vessels. Overgrowth of synovial lesion results eventually in destruction of cartilage and bone. Cytokines play major role in RA.

Synovial fluid Viscous (thick) joint fluid that lubricates joints.

Velvet Soft and highly vascular deciduous substance which envelops and nourishes antlers of deer during their rapid growth.

REFERENCES

Chapter 1 Overture

[1] Yoon P. "The effect of deer horn on the experimental anemia of rabbits." *Journal of Pharmacochemical Society* 1989;8:6-11.
[2] Michael E. Rosenbaum, MD. Personal interview, July 1999.
[3] Lincoln GA, Tyler NJ. "Role of estradiol in the regulation of the seasonal antler cycle in female reindeer." *Journal of Reproduction and Fertility* 1999 Jan;115(1):167-74.
[4] Kong Y, Ko K. "Epidermal growth factor of the cervine velvet antler." *Acta Zoology Sin* 1987;33:301-308.
[5] Yoon P. 1989, op cit.

Chapter 2 From the Caldron to the Health Store

[1] *Deer Antler Velvet*, "A unique renewable source," p 22.
[2] Lincoln GA, Tyler NJ. "Role of estradiol in the regulation of the seasonal antler cycle in female reindeer." *Journal of Reproduction and Fertility* 1999 Jan;115(1):167-74.
[3] Garcia RL et al. "Expression of neurotrophin-3 in the growing velvet antler of the red deer Cervus elaphus." *Journal of Molecular Endocrinology* 1997 Oct;19(2):173-82.
[4] New Zealand Game Industry Board, Technical Manual. "Background."
[5] Matthews, L. Ruakura Res Center, Hamilton, New Zealand, in *Deer Antler Velvet*, p. 12.
[6] Rolf HJ, Enderle A. "Hard fallow deer antler: a living bone till antler casting?" *Anatomical Records* 1999 May 1;255(1):69-77.
[7] *Velvet Antler*, Elk Tech International Research Center, p. 3.
[8] Goss RJ. "Future directions in antler research." *Anatomical Records* 1995 Mar;241:291-302.

Chapter 3 History and Traditions

[1] Fennessy, P. Invermay Research Centre, Otago, New Zealand. Cited in "Promising results from NA studies," in *Deer Velvet.*
[2] Yoon, in *Deer Velvet.*
[3] Suttie, JM; Haines, SR. "Evaluation of New Zealand velvet antler efficacy and diagnostic testing." New Zealand: VARNz Ltd.,1996.
[4] Fisher, BD et al. "Strength training parameters in Edmonton police recruits following supplementation with elk velvet antler (EVA)." University of Alberta. 1998.
[5] Takikawa K et al. "Experimental whiplash injury. 3. Changes in enzyme activities of cervical cord and effect of Pantui extract, pantocrin." *Nippon Yakurigaku Zasshi* 1972 Jul;68:489-93.
[6] Church, J.S. "Velvet Antler: Its historical medical use, performance-enhancing effects and pharmacology." Elk Tech Intnl Research Center, http://www.elk-tech.com/research.htm. 1999.
[7] Yudin, A.M, Dubryakov, YL. "A guide for the preparation and storage of uncalcified male antlers as a medicinal raw material." In: *Reindeer Antlers*, Academy of Sciences of the USSR. Vladivostock: Far East Science Center. 1974.
[8] Fisher 1998, op cit.
[9] Suttie, JM, Haines, S. "G.I.B. component of velvet antler programme: evaluation of velvet antler." New Zealand: VARNz Ltd.,1996.
[10] Sim, JS, Sunwoo, HH. "Canadian scientists study velvet antler for arthritis treatment." *Canadian Elk & Deer Farmer*, Winter 1999;39-40.

Chapter 4 How Does Velvet Antler Work?

[1] Cooper DA et al. "Dietary carotenoids and lung cancer: a review of recent research." *Nutrition Reviews* 1999 May:57(5Pt 1):133-45.

[2] 39th Annual Conference on Cardiovascular Disease Epidemiology and Prevention, Orlando, Florida. Reuter's Health, March 29, 1999.

[3] Ascherio A et al. "Intake of vitamins E, C and carotenoids does not 'substantially' reduce stroke risk." *Annals of Internal Medicine* 1999;130:963-970.

Chapter 5 What's In Velvet Antler?

[1] Sunwoo, HH et al. "Isolation, characterization and localization of glycosamines in growing antlers of wapiti (Cervus elephus)." *Comp Biochemistry and Physiology* Part B1998; 273-283.

[2] Tsjuibo et al. 1987. Technical Manual, New Zealand Game Industry Board.

[3] Wang, B. "Advances in research of chemistry, pharmacology and clinical application of pilose antler." Proc of the 1996 Intnl Symp on Deer Science and Deer Products. 1996; 14-31.

[4] Sunwoo HH et al. 1998, 437-42, op cit

[5] Sunwoo HH et al. 1998, 273-83, op cit.

[6] Fernandez-Botran R et al. "Binding of interferon gamma by glycosaminoglycans: a strategy for localization and/or inhibition of its activity." *Cytokine* 1999 May;11(5):313-25.

[7] Poggi MM et al. "Effects of cryopreservation and deconstruction on the dermal glycosaminoglycan content of human skin." *Jnl of Burn Care and Rehab* 1999 May-Jun;20(3):201-6.

[8] Hedlund H et al. "Association of the aggrecan keratan sulfate-rich region with collagen in bovine articular cartilage." *Journal of Biologic Chemistry* 1999 Feb 26;274(9):5777-81.

[9] Sunwoo, HH et al. "Glycosaminoglycans from growing antlers of wapiti (Cervuselaphus)." *Canadian Journal of Animal Science* 1997; 77: 715-421.

[10] Jhon GJ et al. "Studies of the chemical structure of gangliosides in deer antler, Cervus nippon." *Chemical and Pharmacological Bulletin* (Tokyo) 1999 ;47(1):123-7.

[11] Suttie, JM. *The New Zealand Velvet Antler Industry: Background and Reseach Findings.* Varnz Document V27. New Zealand Game Industry Board, Wellington, New Zealand.

Chapter 6 What's Special About What's In Velvet?

[1] Yasui, N., M.E. Nimni. "Cartilage collagens," in *Collagen*, Vol 1. M.E. Nimmi, ed. Boca Raton: CRC Press. 1998;225-241.

[2] Ibid.

[3] Kalden, JR, Sieper, J. "Oral collagen in the treatment of rheumatoid arthritis." *Arthritis and Rheumatism* 1998;41(2): 191-194.

[4] Price, JS et al. "Chondrogenesis in the regenerating antler tip in red deer: expression of collagen types1,IIA, IIB, and X demonstrated by in situ nucleic acid hybridization and immuno-cytochemistry." *Developing Dynamics* 1996;205(3): 332-347.

[5] Ibid.

[6] Adam M. "Osteoarthrosis therapy with gelatin preparations: Results of a clinical study." *Therapiewoche* 1991;38:2456-2461.

[7] Goetz B. "Chondropathia patellae. *Arztliche Praxis* 1982; 92:3130-3134.

[8] Krug E. "On supportive therapy for osteo- and chondropathies." *Ztschr.f.Ergahrungsheilkunde* 1979;11:930-938.
[9] Oberschelp, U. "Comparative study of 154 patients with Gerontamin and physical therapy. *Therapiewoche* 1985;44:5094-5097.
[10] Seeligmuller, K; Happel, HK. "Can a mixture of gelatin and L-cystine stimulate proteoglycan synthesis?" *Therapiewoche* 1989;39:3153-3157.
[11] Li C, Suttie JM. "Electron microscopic studies of antlerogenic cells from five developmental stages during pedicle and early antler formation in red deer (Cervus elaphus)." *Anatomical Records* 1998 Dec;252(4):587-99.
[12] Rucklidge GJ et al. "Deer antler does not represent a typical endochondral growth system: immunoidentification of collagen type X but little collagen type II in growing antler tissue." *Biology* 1997 Oct;118(2):303-8. Email: gjr@rri.sari.ac.uk.
[13] Szuwart T et al. "Ultrastructural aspects of cartilage formation, mineralization, and degeneration during primary antler growth in fallow deer." *Anat Anz* 1998 Dec;180:501-10.
[14] Sim, JS, Sunwoo, HH. "Canadian scientists study velvet antler for arthritis treatment." *Canadian Elk & Deer Farmer*, Winter 1999;39-40.
[15] Conrozier T. "Anti-arthrosis treatments: efficacy and tolerance of chondroitin sulfates." *Presse Med* 1998;Nov 21;27(36):1862-5.
[16] Sunwoo, HH et al. "Isolation, characterization and localization of glycosamines in growing antlers of wapiti (Cervus elephus)." *Comparative Biochemistry and Physiology* Part B1998: 273-283.Op cit Sunwoo, *Biochemical Physiology*
[17] New Zealand Game Industry Board.
[18] Sunwoo, HH et al. "Glycosaminoglycans from growing antlers of wapiti (Cervuselaphus)." *Canadian Journal of Animal Science* 1997; 77: 715-421.
[19] Sunwoo, HH et al. 1998, op cit.
[20] Francis SM, Suttie JM. "Detection of growth factors and proto-oncogene mRNA in the growing tip of red deer (Cervus elaphus) antler using reverse-transcriptase polymerase chainreaction (RT-PCR)." *Journal of Experimental Zoology* 1998 May 1;281(1):36-42.
[21] Fisher, BD et al. "Strength training parameters in Edmonton police recruits following supplementation with elk velvet antler (EVA)." University of Alberta. 1998.
[22] Kozakowski J et al. *Polish Archives of Medicine* 1998 Oct;100(4):306-12.
[23] Valimaki MJ et al. "Effects of 42 months of GH treatment on bone mineral density and bone turnover in GH-deficient adults." *European Journal of Endocrinology* 1999 Jun;140:545-554.
[24] Rosen CJ, Pollak M. "Circulating IGF-I: New Perspectives for a New Century." *TRENDS IN ENDOCRINOLOGY AND METABOLISM* 1999 MAY;10(4):136-141.
[25] Fennessy, PF. "Antler growth: nutritional and endocrine factors," in: *Biology of Deer Production, 1991*. Wellington Royal Society, New Zealand.
[26] Matteucci BM. "Metabolic and endocrine disease and arthritis." *Current Opinions in Rheumatology* 1995 Jul;7(4):356-8.
[27] Kozakowski J et al. 1998, op cit.
[28] Mineshita, T. "Study of Lu-jung, the Chinese drug VI. Influence of lu-jung on the growth of mice." *Folia Pharamacologica Japonica* 1937;23:221-232.
[29] Suttie JM, Haines, SR. "Evaluation of New Zealand velvet antler efficacy and diagnostic testing." AgResearch, Invermay Agricultural Center, Private Bag 50034, Mosgiel, New Zealand. VARNZ Document V34.

[30]Hoffman AR et al. "Functional consequences of the somatopause and its treatment." *Endocrine* 1997;7(1):73-76.

[31] Kamen B, Kamen S. *The Kamen Plan for Total Nutrition During Pregnancy* 1981. Appleton-Century Crofts, New York, pp 186-7.

[32] Stryer, L. "Fatty Acid Metabolism," in: *Biochemistry*, 4th Ed 1995, W.H. Freeman & Co., NY, p. 624

[33] Weinreb M, Grosskopf A, Shir N. "The anabolic effect of PGE2 in rat bone marrow cultures is mediated via the EP4 receptor subtype." *Amer Jnl of Physiology* 1999 Feb;276(2 Pt 1):E376-83.

[34] Wani MR et al. "Prostaglandin E2 cooperates with TRANCE in osteoclast induction from hemopoietic precursors: synergistic activation of differentiation, cell spreading, and fusion." *Endocrinology* 1999 Apr;140(4):1927-35.

[35] Kajii T et al. "Long-term effects of prostaglandin E2 on the mineralization of a clonal osteoblastic cell line (MC3T3-E1)." *Archives of Oral Biology*1999 Mar;44(3):233-41; kajii@den.hokudai.ac.jp.

[36] Burgio, PA. *Velvet Factors Affecting Growth, Biochemical Analysis and the Medicinal Application.* Research paper on published literature on velvet to determine factors affecting growth, biochemical composition, and medicinal applications.

[37] Church, J.S. "Velvet Antler: Its historical medical use, performance-enhancing effects and pharmacology." Elk Tech Intnl Research Center. http://www.elk-tech.com/research.htm. 1999.

CHAPTER 7 Arthritis

[1] Cunningham SG. "Women's heart health—an integrated approach to prevention." *Canadian Journal of Cardiovascular Nursing* 1998;9(3):28-37.

[2] Theodosakis, J et al. *Arthritis Cure*, St Martin's Press, New York, 1997.

[3] Bautch JC et al. "Effects of exercise on knee joints with osteoarthritis: a pilot study of biologic markers." *Arthritis Care Research* 1997 Feb;10(1):48-55.

[4] Otterness IG et al. "Exercise protects against articular cartilage degeneration in the hamster." *Arthritis Rheum* 1998 Nov;41(11):2068-76.

[5] Firth EC et al. "Galloping exercise induces regional changes in bone density within the third and radial carpal bones of Thoroughbred horses." *Equine Veterinary Jnl* 1999 Mar;31:111-5.

[6] Visser NA et al. "Increase of decorin content in articular cartilage following running." *Connective Tissue Research* 1998;37(3-4):295-302.

[7] Ettrich U, et al. "Overview of the current status of measurable parameters of cartilage metabolism in various body fluids." *Z Rheumatology* 1998 Dec;57(6):375-91.

[8] Simon LS. "Visco supplementation therapy with intra-articular hyaluronic acid. Fact or fantasy?" *Rheumatic Disease Clinic of North America* 1999 May;25(2):345-57.

[9] Aalykke C et al. "Helicobacter pylori and risk of ulcer bleeding among users of nonsteroidal anti-inflammatory drugs: A case-control study." *Gastroenterology* 1999 Jun;116(6):1305-9

[10] Cebollero-Santamaria et al. "Selective outpatient management of upper gastrointestinal bleeding in the elderly." *American Journal of Gastroenterology*1999 May;94(5):1242-7.

[11] Aabakken L. "Small-bowel side-effects of non-steroidal anti-inflammatory drugs." *European Journal of Gastroenterology & Hepatology* 1999 Apr;11(4):383-8.

[12] "Arthritis Foundation urges calm amid new drug safety concerns." Reuters, May 17, 1999.
[13] Conrozier T. "Chondroitin sulfates (chondroitin sulfur 4&6): practical applications and economic impact." *Presse Med* 1998 Nov 21;27(36):1866-8.
[14] Bassleer C et al. "Stimulation of proteoglycan production by glucosamine sulfate in chondrocytes isolated from human osteoarthritic articular cartilage in vitro." *Osteoarthritis Cartilage* 1998 Nov;6(6):427-34.
[15] Theodosakis J et al. 1997 op cit., p 44.
[16] Leffler CT et al. "Glucosamine, chondroitin, and manganese ascorbate for degenerative joint disease of the knee or low back: a randomized, double-blind, placebo-controlled pilot study." *Military Medicine*. 1999 Feb;164(2):85-91.
[17] Haas, EM. *Staying Healthy with Nutrition*, Celestial Arts, Berkeley, California, 1992, p 206.
[18] Michael E. Rosenbaum, MD. Personal interview, June 30, 1999.
[19] Deal CL, Moskowitz RW. "Nutraceuticals as therapeutic agents in osteoarthritis. The role of glucosamine, chondroitin sulfate, and collagen hydrolysate." *Rheumatic Disease Clinics of North America* 1999 May;25(2):379-95.
[20] Russell AL. "Glucosamine in osteoarthritis and gastrointestinal disorders: an exemplar of the need for a paradigm shift." *Medical Hypotheses* 1998 Oct;51:347-9.
[21] McCarty MF. "Enhanced synovial production of hyaluronic acid may explain rapid clinical response to high-dose glucosamine in osteoarthritis." *Medical Hypotheses* 1998 Jun;50:507-10.
[22] Chopra R, Anastassiades T. "Specificity and synergism of polypeptide growth factors in stimulating the synthesis of proteoglycans and a novel high molecular weight anionic glycoprotein by articular chondrocyte cultures." *Journal of Rheumatology* 1998 Aug;25(8):1578-84.
[23] Yudin, A.M, Dubryakov, YL. "A guide for the preparation and storage of uncalcified male antlers as a medicinal raw material." In: *Reindeer Antlers*, Academy of Sciences of thc USSR. Vladivostock: FarEast Science Center. 1974
[24] Wang, B. *Advances in research of chemistry, pharmacology and clinicalapplication of pilose antler.* Proc of the 1996 Intnl Symposium on Deer Science and Deer Products. 1996; 14-31.
[25] Suttie, JM, Haines, S. "G.I.B. component of velvet antler programme: evaluation of velvet antler." New Zealand: VARNz Ltd.,1996.
[26] Morreale P et al. "Comparison of the Anti-inflammatory Efficacy of Chondroitin Sulfate and Diclofenac Sodium in Patients with Knee Osteoarthritis." *Journal of Rheumatology* 1996;23(8):1391.
[27] Kalden, JR, Sieper, J. "Oral collagen in the treatment of rheumatoid arthritis." *Arthritis and Rheumatism* 1998;41(2): 191-194.
[28] Trentham, DE et al. "Effects of oral administration of type II collagen on rheumatoid arthritis." *Science* 1993; 261: 1727-1730.
[29] Kalden, JR, Sieper, J. 1998, op cit.
[30] Ibid.
[31] Trentham DE et al. 1993, op cit. Page?
[32] van den Berg WB. "Joint inflammation and cartilage destruction may occur uncoupled." *Springer Seminars on Immunopathology* 1998;20(1-2):149-64.
[33] Trentham DE et al. 1993, op cit, p 19.

[34]Barnett, M.L. et al. "A pilot trial of oral type II collagen in the treatment of juvenile rheumatoid arthritis." *Arthritis & Rheumatism* 1996; 39 (4): 623-628..
[35] Matsuno H et al. "Biochemical effect of intra-articular injections of high molecular weight hyaluronate in rheumatoid arthritis patients." *Inflammation Res* 1999 Mar;48:154-92):85-91.
[36] Shephard RJ, Shek. "PN Autoimmune disorders, physical activity, and training, with particular reference to rheumatoid arthritis." *Exercise Immunology Revew* 1997;3:53-67.
[37] Evans CH, Robbins PD. "Potential treatment of osteoarthritis by gene therapy." *Rheumatic Disease Clinic of North America* 1999 May;25(2):333-44.

CHAPTER 8 Other Conditions Helped with Velvet

[1] Brekhman, JT et al. The biological activityof the antlers of deer and other deer speicies. *IvestioSibirskogoOrderlemia Akalemi Nank SISR*, Biological Series No 10 (2):112-115.
[2] Yudin, AM, Dubryakov, YL. "A guide for the preparation and storage of uncalcified male antlers as a medicinal raw material." In: *Reindeer Antlers*, Academy of Sciences of the USSR. Vladivostock: FarEast Science Center. 1974
[3] Fulder, S. "The drug that builds Russians." *New Scientist* 1980b;87(1215): 516-519.
[4] Gerrard, D.F et al. "Clinical evaluation of New Zealand deer velvet antler on muscle strength and endurance in healthy male university athletes." Agsearch Invermay, New Zealand.
[5] Bender AS et al. "Effect of lactic acid on L-glutamate uptake in cultured astrocytes: mechanistic considerations." *Brain Research* 1997 Mar 7;750(1-2):59-66.
[6] Fisher, BD et al. "Strength training parameters in Edmonton police recruits following supplementation with elk velvet antler (EVA)." University of Alberta. 1998.
[7] Reidenbach, F. "Estrogen-androgen therapy alters body composition in postmenopausal women." Reuter's, June 23, 1999.
[8] Josephson, D. "Concern raised about performance enhancing drugs in the US." *British Medical Journal* 1998, Sep 12;317:702.
[9] "Transdermal testosterone improves sexual function in oophorectomized women." Data presented at the annual meeting of The Endocrine Society, San Diego. *Reuters Health*, Jun 16, 1999.
[10] Wang, B. Advances in research of chemistry, pharmacology and clinical application of pilose antler. Proc of the 1996 Intnl Symposium on Deer Science and Deer Products. 1996; 14-31.
[11] Church, J.S. "Velvet Antler: Its historical medical use, performance-enhancing effects and pharmacology." Elk Tech International Research Centre, 1999.
[12] Fernandez-Botran R et al. "Binding of interferon gamma by glycosaminoglycans: as strategy for localization and/or inhibition of its activity." *Cytokine* 1999 May;11(5):313-25.
[13] Prudden JF, Balassa, LL. "The biological activity of bovine cartilage preparations." *Seminars on Arthritis and Rheumatism*
1974:3(4):287.
[14] Levine S, Takamoto A. "Immune System Disorders & Supportive Therapies," Carbon Based Seminars Syllabus, May 10 1997.
[15] Prudden JF, Balassa, LL. 1974, op cit.

[16] Hong, ND et al. "Studies on combined usage of combined preparation of crude drugs and anti-neoplastic drugs (II). Alleviating effect of *cis*-Platin and mitomycin C through combined use of gamidaebo tang." *Pharmacognosy* 1992;23:89-95.

CHAPTER 9 Velvet Antler As A Supplement

[1] Website: www.qeva.com/research/naeba.htm.

[2] Burgio, P.A. Velvet: Factors Affecting Growth, Biochemical Analysis, and the Medicinal Application.

[3] Conte A et al. "Biochemical and pharmacokinetic aspects of oral treatment with chondroitin sulfate." *Arxheim-Forsch/Drug Research* 1995;45(11):194.

[4] Palmieri, L et al. "Metabolic fate of exogenous chondroitin sulfate in the experimental animal." *Arzneim-Forsch Drug Research* 1990;40 (1): 319-323.

[5] Kamen B. *Total Nutrition for Breast-Feeding Mothers*. Little, Brown, Boston. 1986. p 9.

[6] Gavrin 1976. New Zealand Game Industry Board

[7] Sim JS, Sunwoo, HH. "Canadian scientists study velvet antler for arthritis treatment." *Canadian Elk & Deer Farmer,* Winter 1999, p. 28.

INDEX